D0069415

GRAVITY AND GLADNESS

The Pursuit of God in Corporate Worship

Study Guide Developed by Desiring God

:: CROSSWAY
WHEATON, ILLINOIS

Gravity AND *Gladness Study Guide*

Copyright © 2010 by Desiring God

Published by Crossway
   1300 Crescent Street
   Wheaton, Illinois 60187

Cover design: Amy Bristow

Cover photo: iStock

First printing 2010

Printed in the United States of America

Italics in biblical quotes indicate emphasis added.

Unless otherwise indicted, Scripture quotations are from the ESV® Bible
(*The Holy Bible, English Standard Version*®), copyright © 2001 by Crossway.
Used by permission. All rights reserved.

Scripture references marked NRSV are from *The New Revised Standard Version*.
Copyright © 1989 by the Division of Christian Education of the National Council
of the Churches of Christ in the U.S.A. Published by Thomas Nelson, Inc. Used by
permission of the National Council of the Churches of Christ in the U.S.A.

ISBN-13: 978-1-4335-1504-0

ISBN-10: 1-4335-1504-0

PDF ISBN: 1-4335-1505-7

Mobipocket ISBN: 1-4335-1506-4

ePub ISBN: 1-4335-2484-4

Crossway is a publishing ministry of Good News Publishers.

VP		19	18	17	16	15	14	13	12	11	10
14	13	12	11	10	9	8	7	6	5	4	3	2	1

CONTENTS

INTRODUCTION TO THIS STUDY GUIDE

IN THE UNITED STATES, contrary to inflated poll numbers, it is estimated that about 20 percent of the population goes to a Christian church on any given Sunday. That is still about sixty *million* people who attend a Christian "worship service" on a Sunday in America. These sixty million people attend as many as five hundred thousand Christian churches.

If there are five hundred thousand Christian churches in the United States, what is happening in those churches during their Sunday morning service or services? What *should* be happening? How should the Christian leaders who are planning and leading those services think about what is happening? What should those who are participating in these worship services think about their participation, and how should they prepare for worship?

In view of these numbers and questions, it is clearly important for Christians to form what may be called a philosophy of corporate worship. That is exactly what this study guide and corresponding seminar is designed to do.

In order to understand how to plan for and participate in corporate worship services, however, we must first ask the crucial question of what worship is. Therefore, much of this seminar and study guide will be devoted to answering this question—to searching for the Bible's teaching on the nature of true worship.

And in our search for the Bible's teaching on worship we will discover that true worship is not only intended for Sunday mornings. God has created us to worship him in all of life, in gravity and in gladness.

This study guide is designed to be used in a twelve-session,[1] guided group study that focuses on the *Gravity and Gladness* DVD Set.[2] After an introductory lesson, each subsequent lesson examines one twenty-five minute session[3] from the *Gravity and Gladness* seminar. You, the learner, are encouraged to prepare for the viewing of each session by reading and reflecting upon Scripture, by considering key quotations, and by asking yourself penetrating questions. Your preparatory work for each lesson is marked with the heading "Before You Watch the DVD, Study and Prepare" in Lessons 2–11.

The workload is conveniently divided into five daily (and manageable) assignments. There is also a section suggesting further study. This work is to be completed individually before the group convenes to view the DVD and discuss the material.

> Throughout this study guide, paragraphs printed in a shaded box like this one are excerpts from a book written by John Piper or excerpts taken from the Desiring God Web site. They are included to supplement the study questions and to summarize key or provocative points.

The second section in Lessons 2–11, entitled "Further Up and Further In," is designed for the learner who wants to explore the concepts and ideas introduced in the lesson in greater detail. This

GRAVITY ᴀɴᴅ GLADNESS

section is not required but will deepen your understanding of the material.

The third section in Lessons 2–11, entitled "While You Watch the DVD, Take Notes," is to be completed as the DVD is playing. This section includes fill-in-the-blanks and leaves space for taking notes. You are encouraged to engage with the DVD by filling in the appropriate blanks and writing down other notes that will aid you in the group discussion.

The fourth section in each normal lesson is "After You Watch the DVD, Discuss What You've Learned." Three discussion questions are provided to guide and focus the conversation. You may record, in the spaces provided, notes that will help you contribute to the conversation. Or you may use this space to record things from the discussion that you want to remember.

The final section is an application section, "After You Discuss, Make Application." You will be challenged to record a "take-away point" and to engage in a certain activity that is a fitting response to the content presented in the lesson.

Group leaders will want to find the "Leader's Guide," included at the end of this study guide, immediately.

Life transformation will only occur by the grace of God. Therefore, we highly encourage you to seek the Lord in prayer throughout the learning process. Pray that God would open your eyes to see wonderful things in his Word. Pray that he would grant you the insight and concentration you need in order to get the most from this resource. Pray that God would cause you not merely to understand the truth but also to rejoice in it. And pray that the discussion in your group would be mutually encouraging and edifying. We've included objectives at the beginning of each lesson.

These objectives won't be realized without the gracious work of God through prayer.

NOTES

1. While this study guide is ideally suited for a twelve-session study, it is possible to complete it in six sessions. For instructions on how to use this study guide for a six-session group study, turn to Appendix A: Six-Session Intensive Option.

2. Although this resource is designed to be used in a group setting, it can also be used by the independent learner. Such a learner would have to decide for himself or herself how to use this resource in the most beneficial way. We would suggest doing everything but the group discussion, if possible.

3. Twenty-five minutes is only an approximation. Some sessions are longer; others are shorter.

LESSON 1
INTRODUCTION TO *GRAVITY AND GLADNESS*

LESSON OBJECTIVES

It is our prayer that after you have finished this lesson . . .

> You will get a feel for how you and others in your group approach the issue of corporate worship.

> Your curiosity will be roused, and questions will begin to come to mind.

> You will be eager to learn more about how you can worship the true God in spirit and in truth.

ABOUT YOURSELF

1) What is your name?

2) Tell the group something about yourself that they probably don't already know.

3) What are you hoping to learn from this group study?

11

A PREVIEW OF *GRAVITY AND GLADNESS*

1) What kinds of Christian worship services have you participated in throughout your life? Describe to the group how these worship services were different from each other. What components did these worship services include, what tone was set in these worship services, and how did the preaching of God's Word relate to the rest of what was done?

2) What, in your mind, are nonnegotiable elements of a corporate, Christian worship service? Is it legitimate to worship God in a variety of styles and forms? If so, how should a church choose its worship style and forms? Explain.

LESSON 2
GRAVITY AND GLADNESS: THE PURSUIT OF
GOD IN CORPORATE WORSHIP
A Companion Study to Gravity and Gladness, *Session 1*

LESSON OBJECTIVES

It is our prayer that after you have finished this lesson . . .

> You will begin to reflect on how you approach corporate worship.

> You will understand the relationship between God's pursuit of us and our pursuit of him.

> You will be able to describe why the title for this study guide includes the words *gravity* and *gladness*.

BEFORE YOU WATCH THE DVD, STUDY AND PREPARE

DAY 1: CORPORATE WORSHIP

This study guide focuses on corporate, Christian worship of God. Corporate worship is the worship Christians engage in when they are assembled with other believers, as opposed to personal, or individual, worship. Most churches meet for corporate worship on Sunday mornings.

*QUESTION 1: List all of the characteristics of "individual worship" and "corporate worship" that you can think of. Push yourself to list both similarities and differences beyond the obvious ones.[1]

Individual Worship	Corporate Worship

Now read Psalm 42:1–6.

PSALM 42:1–6

[1] As a deer pants for flowing streams, so pants my soul for you, O God. [2] My soul thirsts for God, for the living God. When shall

I come and appear before God? [3] My tears have been my food day and night, while they say to me all the day long, "Where is your God?" [4] These things I remember, as I pour out my soul: how I would go with the throng and lead them in procession to the house of God with glad shouts and songs of praise, a multitude keeping festival. [5] Why are you cast down, O my soul, and why are you in turmoil within me? Hope in God; for I shall again praise him, my salvation [6] and my God. . . .

QUESTION 2: What does the psalmist call to mind in order to battle his depression? Why might this be significant?

DAY 2: WHO PURSUES WHOM IN WORSHIP?

The subtitle of this lesson (which is also the subtitle of this seminar) is "The Pursuit of God in Corporate Worship." The phrase "The Pursuit of God" in the subtitle, however, is ambiguous. Does this phrase indicate that corporate worship is *God's* pursuit of *us* or *our* pursuit of *God*?

QUESTION 3: When you hear the phrase "The Pursuit of God in Corporate Worship," does Statement A or Statement B (on the next page) come to mind first? Explain your answer. What might your answer indicate about how you view worship?

Statement A: In corporate worship, God pursues us.

Statement B: In corporate worship, we pursue God.

Study John 4:23, John 15:16, Psalm 105:2–4, and Jeremiah 29:10–13, which will help us think about the question of who pursues whom in worship.

JOHN 4:23

> But the hour is coming, and is now here, when the true worshipers will worship the Father in spirit and truth, for the Father is seeking such people to worship him.

JOHN 15:16

> You did not choose me, but I chose you and appointed you that you should go and bear fruit and that your fruit should abide, so that whatever you ask the Father in my name, he may give it to you.

PSALM 105:2–4

> 2 Sing to him, sing praises to him; tell of all his wondrous works!
> 3 Glory in his holy name; let the hearts of those who seek the

LORD rejoice! ⁴ Seek the LORD and his strength; seek his presence continually!

JEREMIAH 29:10–13

¹⁰ For thus says the LORD: When seventy years are completed for Babylon, I will visit you, and I will fulfill to you my promise and bring you back to this place. ¹¹ For I know the plans I have for you, declares the LORD, plans for welfare and not for evil, to give you a future and a hope. ¹² Then you will call upon me and come and pray to me, and I will hear you. ¹³ You will seek me and find me, when you seek me with all your heart.

*QUESTION 4: According to the four passages cited above, does God pursue us or do we pursue him in our relationship with him? Underline phrases that support your answer, and then record your reflections on this question below.

DAY 3: WHOSE PURSUIT IS FIRST?

In Day 2, we saw that the Bible speaks of us pursuing God *and* of God pursuing us. This observation prompts the question of how these two pursuits are related to each other. Does God pursue us first? Or do we pursue God first? Study Philippians 3:12, reproduced below with its preceding context:

PHILIPPIANS 3:8–12

> 8 Indeed, I count everything as loss because of the surpassing worth of knowing Christ Jesus my Lord. For his sake I have suffered the loss of all things and count them as rubbish, in order that I may gain Christ 9 and be found in him, not having a righteousness of my own that comes from the law, but that which comes through faith in Christ, the righteousness from God that depends on faith—10 that I may know him and the power of his resurrection, and may share his sufferings, becoming like him in his death, 11 that by any means possible I may attain the resurrection from the dead. 12 Not that I have already obtained this or am already perfect, but I press on to make it my own, *because* Christ Jesus has made me his own.

*QUESTION 5: How is Paul's pursuit of Christ related to Christ's pursuit of Paul? Be sure to explain the significance of the word "because" (italicized in verse 12) in your answer.

Examine also 1 Peter 4:10–11.

1 PETER 4:10–11

> 10 As each has received a gift, use it to serve one another, as good stewards of God's varied grace: 11 whoever speaks, as one who speaks oracles of God; whoever serves, as one who serves by the strength that God supplies—in order that in everything God may be glorified through Jesus Christ. To him belong glory and dominion forever and ever. Amen.

QUESTION 6: According to 1 Peter 4:10–11, when we serve others, should we serve in our own strength or in God's strength?

Why? How might your answer apply to the way in which we are to worship God?

DAY 4: THE TONE OF CORPORATE WORSHIP

When we speak of the *tone* of corporate worship, we mean the environment that is created by the manner of expression or style in which God is worshiped. How does the worship service "feel"? What emotions is the service designed to stir up? What words would someone use to describe the worship service to someone else?

*QUESTION 7: What do you think should be the primary tone of corporate, Christian worship? Defend your answer.

Now refer back to how you answered the first preview question of Lesson 1, which had you recall the different worship services you have participated in throughout your life.

QUESTION 8: As you think about worship services in which you have participated in the past, choose one word that best describes the tone of each service. Record these words below.

DAY 5: GOD OUR DREAD AND EXCEEDING JOY

The tone of our corporate worship reflects our vision of what God is like, and what is an appropriate response to his character. So decisions about how to design corporate worship services inevitably involve decisions about what the leaders want to communicate about God to those who come to worship.

Study the following two passages, Isaiah 8:11–14 and Psalm 43:3–4, looking for how a vision of who God is affects how his people should approach him.

ISAIAH 8:11–14

> [11] For the LORD spoke thus to me with his strong hand upon me, and warned me not to walk in the way of this people, saying: [12] "Do not call conspiracy all that this people calls conspiracy, and do not fear what they fear, nor be in dread. [13] But the LORD of hosts, him you shall honor as holy. Let him be your fear, and let him be your dread. [14] And he will become a sanctuary and a stone of offense and a rock of stumbling to both houses of Israel, a trap and a snare to the inhabitants of Jerusalem."

PSALM 43:3–4

> [3] Send out your light and your truth; let them lead me; let them bring me to your holy hill and to your dwelling! [4] Then I will go to the altar of God, to God my exceeding joy, and I will praise you with the lyre, O God, my God.

*QUESTION 9: What tone of worship does Isaiah 8:11–14 call for? What tone of worship does Psalm 43:3–4 call for? How does the tone of worship called for relate to how God is portrayed?

QUESTION 10: Is it possible to maintain the tone that Isaiah 8:11–14 calls for while at the same time setting the tone that Psalm 43:3–4 calls for? How might these two passages be applied to corporate worship services simultaneously?

FURTHER UP AND FURTHER IN

Note: The "Further Up and Further In" section is for those who want to study more. It is a section for further reference and going deeper. The phrase "further up and further in" is borrowed from C. S. Lewis.

The biblical book that has the richest and most profound depictions of corporate worship is probably the book of Revelation. Therefore, as further study for this lesson, we will examine some of the key passages in this book that describe corporate worship.

Study Revelation 4:2–11.

REVELATION 4:2–11

2 At once I was in the Spirit, and behold, a throne stood in heaven, with one seated on the throne. 3 And he who sat there had the appearance of jasper and carnelian, and around the throne was a rainbow that had the appearance of an emerald. 4 Around the throne were twenty-four thrones, and seated on the thrones were twenty-four elders, clothed in white garments, with golden crowns on their heads. 5 From the throne came flashes of lightning, and rumblings and peals of thunder, and before the throne were burning seven torches of fire, which are the seven spirits of God, 6 and before the throne there was as it

were a sea of glass, like crystal. And around the throne, on each side of the throne, are four living creatures, full of eyes in front and behind: [7] the first living creature like a lion, the second living creature like an ox, the third living creature with the face of a man, and the fourth living creature like an eagle in flight. [8] And the four living creatures, each of them with six wings, are full of eyes all around and within, and day and night they never cease to say, "Holy, holy, holy, is the Lord God Almighty, who was and is and is to come!" [9] And whenever the living creatures give glory and honor and thanks to him who is seated on the throne, who lives forever and ever, [10] the twenty-four elders fall down before him who is seated on the throne and worship him who lives forever and ever. They cast their crowns before the throne, saying, [11] "Worthy are you, our Lord and God, to receive glory and honor and power, for you created all things, and by your will they existed and were created."

QUESTION 11: How would you describe the tone of the heavenly worship described in this passage? For what are the worshipers praising God?

Now read Revelation 5:6–14.

REVELATION 5:6–14

[6] And between the throne and the four living creatures and among the elders I saw a Lamb standing, as though it had been slain, with seven horns and with seven eyes, which are the seven spirits of God sent out into all the earth. [7] And he went and took the scroll from the right hand of him who was seated on the throne. [8] And when he had taken the scroll, the four living creatures and the twenty-four elders fell down before the Lamb,

each holding a harp, and golden bowls full of incense, which are the prayers of the saints. ⁹ And they sang a new song, saying, "Worthy are you to take the scroll and to open its seals, for you were slain, and by your blood you ransomed people for God from every tribe and language and people and nation, ¹⁰ and you have made them a kingdom and priests to our God, and they shall reign on the earth." ¹¹ Then I looked, and I heard around the throne and the living creatures and the elders the voice of many angels, numbering myriads of myriads and thousands of thousands, ¹² saying with a loud voice, "Worthy is the Lamb who was slain, to receive power and wealth and wisdom and might and honor and glory and blessing!" ¹³ And I heard every creature in heaven and on earth and under the earth and in the sea, and all that is in them, saying, "To him who sits on the throne and to the Lamb be blessing and honor and glory and might forever and ever!" ¹⁴ And the four living creatures said, "Amen!" and the elders fell down and worshiped.

QUESTION 12: How would you describe the tone of the heavenly worship described in *this* passage? For what are the worshipers praising God (and the Lamb)?

Finally, look through the following medley of texts from the rest of Revelation.

REVELATION 11:16–18

¹⁶ And the twenty-four elders who sit on their thrones before God fell on their faces and worshiped God, ¹⁷ saying, "We give thanks to you, Lord God Almighty, who is and who was, for you have taken your great power and begun to reign. ¹⁸ The nations raged, but your wrath came, and the time for the dead

to be judged, and for rewarding your servants, the prophets and saints, and those who fear your name, both small and great, and for destroying the destroyers of the earth."

REVELATION 15:3–4

3 And they sing the song of Moses, the servant of God, and the song of the Lamb, saying, "Great and amazing are your deeds, O Lord God the Almighty! Just and true are your ways, O King of the nations! 4 Who will not fear, O Lord, and glorify your name? For you alone are holy. All nations will come and worship you, for your righteous acts have been revealed."

REVELATION 19:6–8

6 Then I heard what seemed to be the voice of a great multitude, like the roar of many waters and like the sound of mighty peals of thunder, crying out, "Hallelujah! For the Lord our God the Almighty reigns. 7 Let us rejoice and exult and give him the glory, for the marriage of the Lamb has come, and his Bride has made herself ready; 8 it was granted her to clothe herself with fine linen, bright and pure"—for the fine linen is the righteous deeds of the saints.

QUESTION 13: List below the things for which the worshippers in these passages are praising God. Underline words or phrases in these passages that support your answers. Do these passages depict worship as being given with "gravity" and "gladness"?

QUESTION 14: Should Christian worship services on Sunday mornings resemble the worship that is depicted in Revelation? If not, why not? If so, in what ways? Explain your answer.

QUESTION 15: How does the tone of worship and content of praise at your church compare to what you've studied in the book of Revelation?

WHILE YOU WATCH THE DVD, TAKE NOTES

COMMENTS ON THE TITLE OF THE SEMINAR

"Corporate worship"

"Pursuit"

"He took the _____. He's first; I'm second. That's absolutely crucial. Otherwise, he won't get the _____ in our worship."

"Gravity"

"And I just plead with you from all the churches that you come from to be an advocate to move away from _____ on Sunday morning toward _____ _____."

"Gladness"

AFTER YOU WATCH THE DVD, DISCUSS WHAT YOU'VE LEARNED

1) What are the dangers of a worship service that has gravity but lacks gladness? What are the dangers of a worship service that has gladness but lacks gravity?

2) Why is Piper so opposed to worship services that are "chipper"? What does a "chipper" worship service communicate about God, and how does it affect our pursuit of God in corporate worship?

3) Which illustration more effectively communicated to you the simultaneous realities of gravity and gladness—the big dog illustration or the hurricane illustration? Can you think of an illustration from your own experience that would communicate both gravity and gladness?

AFTER YOU DISCUSS, MAKE APPLICATION

1) What was the most meaningful part of this lesson for you? Was there a sentence, concept, or idea that really struck you? Why? Record your thoughts in the space below.

2) What are some practical ways in which you can remind yourself on Sunday mornings that your pursuit of God is dependent upon God's pursuit of you? List some of your ideas below, and describe how these ideas could help you bring glory to God.

NOTES

1. Questions marked with an asterisk (*) are questions that we deem to be particularly significant. If your group is completing this study using the six-session intensive option, we recommend that you complete these questions first and then, if time permits, complete the remaining questions. For more information, see Appendix A—Six-Session Intensive Option.

LESSON 3
WORSHIP ACCORDING TO THE NEW TESTAMENT
A Companion Study to Gravity and Gladness, *Session 2*

LESSON OBJECTIVES

It is our prayer that after you have finished this lesson . . .

- › You will be able to explain the relationship between corporate Christian gatherings and worship.
- › You will be able to describe how the New Testament brings a new understanding of worship.
- › You will better understand the key passage of John 4:20–24.

BEFORE YOU WATCH THE DVD, STUDY AND PREPARE

DAY 1: ARE "WORSHIP SERVICES" BIBLICAL?

There can be little debate that early Christians met together regularly. There is even some evidence in the New Testament that Christians met for some kind of "service" (as we will see below). But what does the New Testament have to say about these gatherings or "services"?

*QUESTION 1: Look at each of the following verses in their contexts. Record any observations you can make on what these verses say about the corporate gatherings of early Christians.

1 Corinthians 11:18

1 Corinthians 14:19, 28

1 Corinthians 14:23

Hebrews 10:25

James 2:2–4

QUESTION 2: Do any of these verses describe these corporate gatherings as "worship services" or even "worship"? What might be the significance of this observation?

DAY 2: WORSHIP IN THE OLD TESTAMENT

How is the word *worship* used in the Bible? We often bring our own understanding of what worship is to the word, but let's see how the Bible itself uses the word. We begin by looking at worship in the Old Testament.

DEUTERONOMY 12:2–6

> 2 You shall surely destroy all the places where the nations whom you shall dispossess served their gods, on the high mountains and on the hills and under every green tree. 3 You shall tear down their altars and dash in pieces their pillars and burn their Asherim with fire. You shall chop down the carved images of their gods and destroy their name out of that place. 4 You shall not *worship* the LORD your God in that way. 5 But you shall seek the place that the LORD your God will choose out of all your tribes to put his name and make his habitation there. There you shall go, 6 and there you shall bring your burnt offerings and your sacrifices, your tithes and the contribution that you present, your vow offerings, your freewill offerings, and the firstborn of your herd and of your flock.

QUESTION 3: How do these verses describe worship? Is the place of worship important in the Old Testament? Explain.

PSALM 95:6

> Oh come, let us worship [Hebrew: *hishtahava*] and bow down; let us kneel before the LORD, our Maker!

2 KINGS 5:14–19

> 14 So he went down and dipped himself seven times in the Jordan, according to the word of the man of God, and his flesh

was restored like the flesh of a little child, and he was clean. [15] Then he returned to the man of God, he and all his company, and he came and stood before him. And he said, "Behold, I know that there is no God in all the earth but in Israel; so accept now a present from your servant." [16] But he said, "As the LORD lives, before whom I stand, I will receive none." And he urged him to take it, but he refused. [17] Then Naaman said, "If not, please let there be given to your servant two mules' load of earth, for from now on your servant will not offer burnt offering or sacrifice to any god but the LORD. [18] In this matter may the LORD pardon your servant: when my master goes into the house of Rimmon to worship [Hebrew: *hishtahava*] there, leaning on my arm, and I bow myself [Hebrew: *hishtahava*] in the house of Rimmon, when I bow myself [Hebrew: *hishtahava*] in the house of Rimmon, the LORD pardon your servant in this matter." [19] He said to him, "Go in peace."

*QUESTION 4: From these two passages, what can you observe about the main Hebrew word for worship, *hishtahava*?

DAY 3: AN ASTONISHING OBSERVATION

The main Hebrew word for worship, *hishtahava*, occurs 171 times in the Old Testament. Of those 171 occurrences in the Greek translation of the Old Testament, it is translated by the Greek word *proskuneo* 164 of those 171 times. Therefore we might expect that this Greek word for *worship* would occur all over the New Testament. But when we look at where and how often *proskuneo* occurs in the New Testament, something astonishing appears.

Occurrences of the Word *Proskuneo* in the New Testament

The Gospels	Book of Acts	Paul's Epistles	Other Epistles	Revelation
Matthew 2:2, 8, 11; 4:9, 10; 8:2; 9:18; 14:33; 15:25; 18:26; 20:20; 28:9, 17; Mark 5:6; 15:19; Luke 4:7, 8; 24:52; John 4:20–24; 9:38; 12:20	Acts 7:43; 8:27; 10:25; 24:11	1 Corinthians 14:25	Hebrews 1:6; 11:21	Revelation 3:9; 4:10; 5:14; 7:11; 9:20; 11:1, 16; 13:4, 8, 12, 15; 14:7, 9, 11; 15:4; 16:2; 19:4, 10, 20; 20:4; 22:8, 9
26 times total	**4 times total**	**1 time total**	**2 times total**	**21 times total**

*QUESTION 5: What are your first impressions upon seeing where in the New Testament the term *proskuneo* ("worship") occurs and how often it occurs?

QUESTION 6: Take the time to look up a sampling of these occurrences (listed above). Do you notice anything about how the word is used in the New Testament?

DAY 4: JESUS, THE TEMPLE, AND WORSHIP

In our attempt to understand what the New Testament teaches about worship, and how worship is viewed differently in the New Testament than in the Old Testament, let's consider the teaching of Jesus.

Remember that in the Old Testament, the temple was the central place of worship. In view of this fact, what is so shocking about Jesus' teaching in the following passages?

MARK 11:15–17

> [15] And they came to Jerusalem. And he entered the temple and began to drive out those who sold and those who bought in the temple, and he overturned the tables of the money-changers and the seats of those who sold pigeons. [16] And he would not allow anyone to carry anything through the temple. [17] And he was teaching them and saying to them, "Is it not written, 'My house shall be called a house of prayer for all the nations'? But you have made it a den of robbers."

MATTHEW 12:1–8

> [1] At that time Jesus went through the grainfields on the Sabbath. His disciples were hungry, and they began to pluck heads of grain and to eat. [2] But when the Pharisees saw it, they said to him, "Look, your disciples are doing what is not lawful to do on the Sabbath." [3] He said to them, "Have you not read what David did when he was hungry, and those who were with him: [4] how he entered the house of God and ate the bread of the Presence, which it was not lawful for him to eat nor for those who were with him, but only for the priests? [5] Or have you not read in the Law how on the Sabbath the priests in the temple profane the Sabbath and are guiltless? [6] I tell you, something greater than the temple is here. [7] And if you had known what this means, 'I desire mercy, and not sacrifice,' you would not have condemned the guiltless. [8] For the Son of Man is lord of the Sabbath."

JOHN 2:18–22

> [18] So the Jews said to him, "What sign do you show us for doing these things?" [19] Jesus answered them, "Destroy this temple, and in three days I will raise it up." [20] The Jews then said, "It has taken forty-six years to build this temple, and will you raise it up in three days?" [21] But he was speaking about the temple of his body. [22] When therefore he was raised from the dead, his disciples remembered that he had said this, and they believed the Scripture and the word that Jesus had spoken.

QUESTION 7: How would you summarize what Jesus taught about the temple in these three passages?

*QUESTION 8: What does Jesus' teaching about the temple have to do with worship?

Do you find it as significant as I do that King David, the greatest worship leader of the Old Testament, wrote all his psalms, sang all his songs, chose all his choirmasters, led all his processions, and gave us the great biblical model for God-centered worship, before Israel had any building they could enter for worship? It was his son Solomon who built the temple, not David. The great period of Israel's creative, powerful, God-centered worship was during the reign of her poet-king David before there was any temple where the people could gather.

What's the significance of this clear historical, biblical fact? The significance seems to be at least this: the temple that Solomon built was not essential for Israel's worship.[1]

DAY 5: THE NEW HOUR FOR WORSHIP

Perhaps the single most important New Testament passage on the topic of worship is John 4:19–24. Study these verses carefully.

JOHN 4:19–24

[19] The woman said to him, "Sir, I perceive that you are a prophet. [20] Our fathers worshiped on this mountain, but you say that in Jerusalem is the place where people ought to worship." [21] Jesus said to her, "Woman, believe me, the hour is coming when neither on this mountain nor in Jerusalem will you worship the Father. [22] You worship what you do not know; we worship what we know, for salvation is from the Jews. [23] But the hour is coming, and is now here, when the true worshipers will worship the Father in spirit and truth, for the Father is seeking such people to worship him. [24] God is spirit, and those who worship him must worship in spirit and truth."

Notice the Samaritan woman's question set next to Jesus' response:

"Our fathers worshiped on this *mountain*, but you say that in *Jerusalem* is the place where people ought to worship."

"Woman, believe me, the hour is coming when neither on this *mountain* nor in *Jerusalem* will you worship the Father. . . . True worshipers will worship the Father in *spirit* and *truth*."

QUESTION 9: What is the relationship between the terms italicized above? Does Jesus enter into the debate about the correct place of worship?

*QUESTION 10: What does it mean to worship the Father "in spirit and truth"?

FURTHER UP AND FURTHER IN

Read or listen to John Piper, "Worship God! (1997)," an online sermon at the Desiring God Web site.[2]

QUESTION 11: Create a basic outline of this sermon as you read or listen to it.

QUESTION 12: What material in this sermon was review for you? What material was new?

Think over the following analogy to worship that Piper makes in his book *Desiring God*:

> Perhaps we can tie things together with this picture: The fuel of worship is the truth of God; the furnace of worship is the spirit of man; and the heat of worship is the vital affections of reverence, contrition, trust, gratitude, and joy.
>
> But there is something missing from this picture. There is furnace, fuel, and heat, but no *fire*. The fuel of truth in the furnace of our spirit does not automatically produce the heat of worship. There must be ignition and fire. This is the Holy Spirit. . . .
>
> Now we can complete our picture. The fuel of worship is a true vision of the greatness of God; the fire that makes the fuel burn white hot is the quickening of the Holy Spirit; the furnace made alive and warm by the flame of truth is our renewed spirit; and the resulting heat of our affections is powerful worship, pushing its way out in confessions, longings, acclamations, tears, songs, shouts, bowed heads, lifted hands, and obedient lives.[3]

QUESTION 13: How would you explain this analogy line by line to someone who couldn't understand what Piper is claiming? Write your own explanatory paraphrase next to each part of Piper's analogy:

the fuel of worship is the truth of God

the furnace of worship is the spirit of man

the heat of worship is the vital affections

the fire of worship is the Holy Spirit

Piper's understanding of worship is not shared by all Christians. Some Christian pastors and worship leaders might have a different understanding of what worship is.

QUESTION 14: Rewrite Piper's analogy by substituting different parts to the analogy according to what you think are popular ideas about Christian worship.

the fuel of worship is the _____

the furnace of worship is the _____

the heat of worship is the _____

the fire of worship is the _____

QUESTION 15: Compare the differences between Piper's analogy and the analogy you constructed according to popular ideas about Christian worship. How would the different understandings of what worship is (as expressed in these different analogies) affect the way in which a worship service was designed and led?

WHILE YOU WATCH THE DVD, TAKE NOTES

THE INTENSIFICATION OF WORSHIP AS AN INWARD EXPERIENCE OF THE HEART

Thesis:

The essential, vital, indispensable, defining heart of worship is the _____ of being satisfied with _____ because God is most glorified in us when we are most satisfied in him. The chief end of man is to glorify God *by* enjoying him forever.

Problem:

Aim:

Observation:

In the New Testament there is very little instruction that deals explicitly with _____ worship—what we call worship _____. There were corporate gatherings, but they are not called "_____."

Question:

Answer:

John 4:20–24

AFTER YOU WATCH THE DVD, DISCUSS WHAT YOU'VE LEARNED

1) Is Piper's definition of the heart of worship a new idea to you? Do you agree with him? Why or why not?

2) If you were to randomly interview ten evangelical Christians on the street, how do you think they would answer the question of what worship is? In what ways might their answers be deficient or biblically inaccurate?

3) Why might Piper be focusing so much time in this seminar to clarifying what true worship is? Wouldn't it be more productive to talk about the issues of style that create the so-called "worship wars"?

AFTER YOU DISCUSS, MAKE APPLICATION

1) What was the most meaningful part of this lesson for you? Was there a sentence, concept, or idea that really struck you? Why? Record your thoughts in the space below.

2) Interview a Christian friend of yours who isn't in this study group, asking him or her the following three questions: What does the Bible teach about what Christians should do together on Sunday mornings?

What did Jesus teach on the topic of worship?

What is at the heart of worship? In other words, what distinguishes true worship from false or fake worship?

Record your friend's answers. (If you have time after the interview, share with him or her what you've learned thus far in this course.)

NOTES

1. John Piper, "I Will Sing Praises to You Among the Nations," an on-line sermon at the Desiring God Web site (www.desiringGod.org). Throughout this study guide we will only provide titles (and not the full Web addresses) for online articles and sermons at the Desiring God Web site. Use the Title Index of the Resource Library to locate these resources.

2. Another sermon by the same title was preached in 1991. For this assignment, listen to the 1997 sermon.

3. John Piper, 82.

LESSON 4
THE BOYCOTT OF "WORSHIP"
A Companion Study to Gravity and Gladness, *Session 3*

LESSON OBJECTIVES

It is our prayer that after you have finished this lesson . . .

> › You will be able to explain why the word *worship* was virtually boycotted by many of the New Testament writers.

> › You will understand why the Bible can call all of life worship.

> › You will see the continuity between John Piper's teaching and the Reformed and Puritan tradition.

BEFORE YOU WATCH THE DVD, STUDY AND PREPARE

DAY 1: RESTATING THE QUESTION

This lesson builds upon the previous one. We will continue to examine John Piper's thesis concerning the "intensification of worship as an inward experience of the heart." Here, again, is Piper's thesis:

> The essential, vital, indispensable, defining heart of worship is the experience of being satisfied with God because God is most glorified in us when we are most satisfied in him. The chief end of man is to glorify God *by* enjoying him for ever.[1]

In the previous lesson, we raised the question of what happened to the main word for *worship* in the Old Testament. We noted that the distribution of the word's occurrences in the New Testament was surprising.

QUESTION 1: Review your answers to Questions 3, 4, 5, and 6 in Lesson 3. What "problem" does one encounter in attempting to understand what the New Testament teaches about worship?

*QUESTION 2: Why might the word *proskuneo* occur only seven times in the New Testament outside of the Gospels and Revelation? Why might Peter, James, John, and Paul have "boycotted" this word in the letters they wrote to the churches?

DAY 2: OTHER WORDS AND LANGUAGE FOR WORSHIP

Another important word on the topic of worship in the Greek translation of the Old Testament is *latreuo*. Unlike *proskuneo*, however, it is often translated as "serve," as in Exodus 23:24, Deuteronomy 8:19, and Daniel 3:12.

EXODUS 23:23–24

²³ When my angel goes before you and brings you to the Amorites and the Hittites and the Perizzites and the Canaanites, the Hivites and the Jebusites, and I blot them out, ²⁴ you shall not bow down [*proskuneo*] to their gods nor serve [*latreuo*] them, nor do as they do, but you shall utterly overthrow them and break their pillars in pieces.

DEUTERONOMY 8:19

And if you forget the LORD your God and go after other gods and serve [*latreuo*] them and worship [*proskuneo*] them, I solemnly warn you today that you shall surely perish.

DANIEL 3:12

There are certain Jews whom you have appointed over the affairs of the province of Babylon: Shadrach, Meshach, and Abednego. These men, O king, pay no attention to you; they do not serve [*latreuo*] your gods or worship [*proskuneo*] the golden image that you have set up.

Now we will examine two New Testament passages in which this word is used:

ROMANS 1:9–10

9 For God is my witness, whom I serve [*latreuo*] with my spirit in the gospel of his Son, that without ceasing I mention you 10 always in my prayers, asking that somehow by God's will I may now at last succeed in coming to you.

PHILIPPIANS 3:3

For we are the circumcision, who worship [*latreuo*] by the Spirit of God and glory in Christ Jesus and put no confidence in the flesh.

The noun form of the verb *latreuo* occurs in the well-known verse of Romans 12:1.

ROMANS 12:1

I appeal to you therefore, brothers, by the mercies of God, to present your bodies as a living sacrifice, holy and acceptable to God, which is your spiritual worship [*latreia*].

*QUESTION 3: Based on these three passages, how would you describe the New Testament's use of the word *latreuo*? How does it compare with the New Testament's use of the word *proskuneo*? (See your answer to Question 6 of Lesson 3, if necessary.)

In the Old Testament, the concept of worship is closely tied to the temple (or tabernacle), priests, and sacrifices. Again, though, when we come to the New Testament, we see a shift in the understanding of what it means to worship God.

Inspect Hebrews 13:10–16.

HEBREWS 13:10–16

[10] We have an altar from which those who serve the tent have no right to eat. [11] For the bodies of those animals whose blood is brought into the holy places by the high priest as a *sacrifice* for sin are burned outside the camp. [12] So Jesus also suffered outside the gate in order to sanctify the people through his own blood. [13] Therefore let us go to him outside the camp and bear the reproach he endured. [14] For here we have no lasting city, but we seek the city that is to come. [15] Through him then let us continually offer up a *sacrifice* of praise to God, that is, the fruit of lips that acknowledge his name. [16] Do not neglect to do good and to share what you have, for such *sacrifices* are pleasing to God.

QUESTION 4: Examine the three uses of the word "sacrifice(s)" in this passage. What is interesting about the last two uses compared to the first use? What might this observation have to do with New Testament worship?

DAY 3: ALL OF LIFE IS WORSHIP

The title of this day's study is simply the conclusion we may draw from what we've been studying. Worship is not confined to a time (Sunday mornings, for example) or a place (a church building). It should be a reality for the believer every hour of every day and in every place. We've already seen that Jesus teaches this reality:

JOHN 4:21–24

21 Jesus said to her, "Woman, believe me, the hour is coming when neither on this mountain nor in Jerusalem will you worship the Father. 22 You worship what you do not know; we worship what we know, for salvation is from the Jews. 23 But the hour is coming, and is now here, when the true worshipers will worship the Father in spirit and truth, for the Father is seeking such people to worship him. 24 God is spirit, and those who worship him must worship in spirit and truth."

Therefore, in everything we do, we may worship God and glorify him.

1 CORINTHIANS 10:31

So, whether you eat or drink, or whatever you do, do all to the glory of God.

COLOSSIANS 3:16–17

16 Let the word of Christ dwell in you richly, teaching and admonishing one another in all wisdom, singing psalms and hymns and spiritual songs, with thankfulness in your hearts to God. 17 And whatever you do, in word or deed, do everything in the name of the Lord Jesus, giving thanks to God the Father through him.

*QUESTION 5: How can the believer make all of life worship?

QUESTION 6: Which of the following statements best described your view of worship before you began this study? Explain your choice.

    a. Worship is what I do when I sing hymns or praise songs to God.

    b. Worship is what I do on Sunday mornings with other believers.

    c. Worship involves raising my hands, closing my eyes, and swaying back and forth.

    d. Worship is cherishing God in my heart in all of life.

DAY 4: AGAIN, ALL OF LIFE IS WORSHIP

We must stress again that the New Testament teaches that all of life is to be worship. So whatever worship is, it cannot be identified with outward forms or places.

As we've read, Paul describes the Christian's bodily existence, presented to God, as an act of worship.

ROMANS 12:1

> I appeal to you therefore, brothers, by the mercies of God, to present your bodies as a living sacrifice, holy and acceptable to God, which is your spiritual worship.

Here is another passage describing what it means to "worship in spirit" (John 4:24).

EPHESIANS 5:18–21

¹⁸ And do not get drunk with wine, for that is debauchery, but be filled with the Spirit, ¹⁹ addressing one another in psalms and hymns and spiritual songs, singing and making melody to the Lord *with your heart*, ²⁰ giving thanks *always* and for everything to God the Father in the name of our Lord Jesus Christ, ²¹ submitting to one another out of reverence for Christ.

*QUESTION 7: What is the significance of the two italicized phrases above? What do these phrases teach us about worship?

We've seen in both Colossians 3:17 and Ephesians 5:20 the idea of "giving thanks to God" as an expression of worship. Another passage with this same idea is Hebrews 12:28. Compare two translations of this verse below.

HEBREWS 12:28 (ENGLISH STANDARD VERSION)

Therefore let us be grateful for receiving a kingdom that cannot be shaken, and thus let us offer to God acceptable worship, with reverence and awe.

HEBREWS 12:28 (NEW REVISED STANDARD VERSION)

Therefore, since we are receiving a kingdom that cannot be shaken, let us give thanks, by which we offer to God an acceptable worship with reverence and awe.

In this particular verse, the New Revised Standard Version translates the original Greek more literally. Notice that it says that we offer God acceptable worship by (or through) thanks (or gratitude).

QUESTION 8: According to this verse, what is the relationship between gratitude and worship? What implications does this verse have for our thinking about everyday life?

DAY 5: CALVIN AND LUTHER ON WORSHIP

This emphasis on the inward experience of worship was recaptured in the Reformed tradition. In this day's study we will consider quotations from John Calvin and Martin Luther. John Piper will discuss these quotations in the DVD session that accompanies this lesson.

Here is a quote from John Calvin:

> [The Master] did not will in outward discipline and ceremonies to prescribe in detail what we ought to do (because he foresaw that this depended on the state of the times, and he did not deem one form suitable for all ages). . . . Because he has taught nothing specifically, and because these things are not necessary to salvation, and for the upbuilding of the church ought to be variously accommodated to the customs of each nation and age, it will be fitting (as the advantage of the church will require) to change and abrogate traditional practices and to establish new ones. Indeed, I admit that we ought not to charge into innovation rashly, suddenly, for insufficient cause. But love will best judge what may hurt or edify; and if we let love be our guide, all will be safe.[2]

*QUESTION 9: Summarize this quotation from Calvin in your own words.

And here is a quote from Martin Luther:

> The worship of God . . . should be free at table, in private rooms, downstairs, upstairs, at home, abroad, in all places, by all people, at all times. Whoever tells you anything else is lying as badly as the pope and the devil himself.[3]

QUESTION 10: What might Luther have been reacting to in this quotation?

FURTHER UP AND FURTHER IN

Jesus' encounter with the Pharisees and the teaching of his disciples in Matthew 15:1–20 is an important episode to consider in our study of what true worship is.

MATTHEW 15:1–20

[1] Then Pharisees and scribes came to Jesus from Jerusalem and said, [2] "Why do your disciples break the tradition of the elders? For they do not wash their hands when they eat." [3] He

answered them, "And why do you break the commandment of God for the sake of your tradition? [4] For God commanded, 'Honor your father and your mother,' and, 'Whoever reviles father or mother must surely die.' [5] But you say, 'If anyone tells his father or his mother, "What you would have gained from me is given to God," [6] he need not honor his father.' So for the sake of your tradition you have made void the word of God. [7] You hypocrites! Well did Isaiah prophesy of you, when he said: [8] 'This people honors me with their lips, but their heart is far from me; [9] in vain do they worship me, teaching as doctrines the commandments of men.'" [10] And he called the people to him and said to them, "Hear and understand: [11] it is not what goes into the mouth that defiles a person, but what comes out of the mouth; this defiles a person." [12] Then the disciples came and said to him, "Do you know that the Pharisees were offended when they heard this saying?" [13] He answered, "Every plant that my heavenly Father has not planted will be rooted up. [14] Let them alone; they are blind guides. And if the blind lead the blind, both will fall into a pit." [15] But Peter said to him, "Explain the parable to us." [16] And he said, "Are you also still without understanding? [17] Do you not see that whatever goes into the mouth passes into the stomach and is expelled? [18] But what comes out of the mouth proceeds from the heart, and this defiles a person. [19] For out of the heart come evil thoughts, murder, adultery, sexual immorality, theft, false witness, slander. [20] These are what defile a person. But to eat with unwashed hands does not defile anyone."

QUESTION 11: What makes the worship of the Pharisees vain? Record your answer below, and underline words and phrases in the passage above that support your answer.

QUESTION 12: What does this passage indirectly teach about the nature of true worship?

Examine Philippians 1:20–24.

PHILIPPIANS 1:20–24

[20] . . . as it is my eager expectation and hope that I will not be at all ashamed, but that with full courage now as always Christ will be honored in my body, whether by life or by death. [21] For to me to live is Christ, and to die is gain. [22] If I am to live in the flesh, that means fruitful labor for me. Yet which I shall choose I cannot tell. [23] I am hard pressed between the two. My desire is to depart and be with Christ, for that is far better. [24] But to remain in the flesh is more necessary on your account.

> Notice from verse 20 what Paul's mission in life is. . . .What Paul is saying is that his earnest hope and passion is that what he does with his body, whether in life or death, will always be worship. In life and death his mission is to magnify Christ—to show that Christ is magnificent, to exalt Christ, and demonstrate that he is great.[4]

QUESTION 13: If Paul's desire is to live a life of worship, how will he do it? Study the context of Philippians 1:20, and notice the word "for" at the beginning of verse 21.

If you have ever wondered where I get the slogan: "God is most glorified in us when we are most satisfied in him," this is the place. Christ is magnified in my death, when in my death I am satisfied with him—when I experience death as gain because I gain him. Or another way to say it is that the essence of praising Christ is prizing Christ. Christ will be praised in my death, if in my death he is prized above life. The inner essence of worship is prizing Christ. Cherishing him, treasuring him, being satisfied with him.[5]

Before you watch the DVD session for this lesson, think over the following two questions and record your thoughts.

QUESTION 14: What would you say to someone who professed Christ but didn't see the need to go to church? Why is *corporate* worship important if all of life is worship?

QUESTION 15: Does it matter whether Piper's teaching about worship is in line with the Reformed and Puritan tradition? Why?

WHILE YOU WATCH THE DVD, TAKE NOTES

Question: Why is *proskuneo* virtually boycotted by some New Testament authors?

Answer: The word did not make clear enough the _____, _____ nature of true worship.

Confirmation:

latreuo

language of the temple:

All of life to the glory of God:

The Reformed and Puritan tradition:

John Calvin

Luther

the Puritans

Conclusion: In the New Testament there is a stunning indifference to the outward _____ and _____ of worship. And there is at the same time a radical intensification of worship as an _____, _____ experience that has no bounds and pervades all of life.

AFTER YOU WATCH THE DVD, DISCUSS WHAT YOU'VE LEARNED

1) Does Piper's conclusion to this session follow from the evidence he's examined? In other words, is Piper's conclusion a legitimate one to draw from the Bible's teaching? Defend your answer.

2) What might be the danger of saying something like, "Worship is very important to me. I worship every Sunday morning at my church"?

3) Why might Christian teachers in every generation have to fight to recapture the inward and spiritual nature of true worship?

AFTER YOU DISCUSS, MAKE APPLICATION

1) What was the most meaningful part of this lesson for you? Was there a sentence, concept, or idea that really struck you? Why? Record your thoughts in the space below.

2) Think of one area of your life that you are not used to viewing as being a possible channel for worship. How might you glorify God in this area of your life? Write down some practical ideas to help you worship him.

NOTES

1. This excerpt is taken from the *Gravity and Gladness* seminar notes, available at the Desiring God Web site.

2. John Calvin, *Institutes of the Christian Religion*, as quoted by John Piper in the *Gravity and Gladness* seminar notes.

3. Martin Luther, as quoted by John Piper in the *Gravity and Gladness* seminar notes.

4. John Piper, "The Inner Essence of Worship," an online sermon at the Desiring God Web site.

5. Ibid.

LESSON 5
WHOM DOES GOD WORSHIP?
A Companion Study to Gravity and Gladness, *Session 4*

LESSON OBJECTIVES

It is our prayer that after you have finished this lesson . . .

> › You will be able to identify the reason why God does all that he does.
>
> › You will understand the difference between being God-centered and self-centered.
>
> › You will be able to relate God's pursuit of his own glory and our pursuit of joy.

BEFORE YOU WATCH THE DVD, STUDY AND PREPARE

DAY 1: WHAT IS THE CHIEF END OF GOD?

At the beginning of this lesson we return again to Piper's overarching thesis:

The essential, vital, indispensable, defining heart of worship is the experience of being satisfied with God because God is most glorified in us when we are most satisfied in him. The chief end of man is to glorify God *by* enjoying him for ever.[1]

Notice in this thesis Piper's assertion that the chief end of man is to glorify God. In order to provide a rock-solid foundation for this end or purpose of man, let's ask another question: What is the chief end of God?

*QUESTION 1: What's your initial response to this question? What *is* the chief end of God?

Obviously, whatever answer we give to Question 1 must find support in the Bible.

QUESTION 2: How would you support your answer to Question 1 from the Bible? Can you think of key verses or passages that you could cite? List these passages below with an explanation as to how these passages support your answer to Question 1.

DAY 2: GOD'S PURSUIT OF *HIS OWN* GLORY

The answer that this study guide will offer to Question 1 is that God's chief end is the same as man's chief end: to glorify God. In this day's study we will examine a number of biblical texts to see if this is true.

ISAIAH 43:6–7

> ⁶ I will say to the north, Give up, and to the south, Do not withhold; bring my sons from afar and my daughters from the end of the earth, ⁷ everyone who is called by my name, whom I created for my glory, whom I formed and made.

JEREMIAH 13:7–11

> ⁷ Then I went to the Euphrates, and dug, and I took the loincloth from the place where I had hidden it. And behold, the loincloth was spoiled; it was good for nothing. ⁸ Then the word of the LORD came to me: ⁹ "Thus says the LORD: Even so will I spoil the pride of Judah and the great pride of Jerusalem. ¹⁰ This evil people, who refuse to hear my words, who stubbornly follow their own heart and have gone after other gods to serve them and worship them, shall be like this loincloth, which is good for nothing. ¹¹ For as the loincloth clings to the waist of a man, so I made the whole house of Israel and the whole house of Judah cling to me, declares the LORD, that they might be for me a people, a name, a praise, and a glory, but they would not listen."

*QUESTION 3: According to these two passages, why does God create and elect his people Israel? Underline words or phrases that support your answer.

ISAIAH 48:9–11

> [9] For my name's sake I defer my anger, for the sake of my praise I restrain it for you, that I may not cut you off. [10] Behold, I have refined you, but not as silver; I have tried you in the furnace of affliction. [11] For my own sake, for my own sake, I do it, for how should my name be profaned? My glory I will not give to another.

QUESTION 4: Underline every mention of God's motivation for doing what he does. Then record below your reflections on what you have underlined.

Worship is what we were created for. This is the final end of all existence: the worship of God. God created the universe so that it would display the worth of his glory. And he created us so that we would see this glory and reflect it by knowing and loving it—with all our heart and soul and mind and strength.[2]

DAY 3: GOD'S INFINITE EXUBERANCE FOR *GOD*

As we've seen, God is in a passionate, unrelenting, unstoppable pursuit of his own glory. All that he does is designed to display the glory of God. Therefore, we might say that our exuberance for God in worship is grounded by God's own infinite exuberance for himself. John 17:24 speaks of this God-centered delight within the Trinity.

JOHN 17:24

> Father, I desire that they also, whom you have given me, may be with me where I am, to see my glory that you have given me because you loved me before the foundation of the world.

Notice that Jesus wants *us* to share in this unspeakably magnificent intra-Trinitarian love. Now read 2 Thessalonians 1:9–10.

2 THESSALONIANS 1:9–10

> [9] They will suffer the punishment of eternal destruction, away from the presence of the Lord and from the glory of his might, [10] when he comes on that day to be glorified in his saints, and to be marveled at among all who have believed, because our testimony to you was believed.

QUESTION 5: What similarities can you observe between John 17:24 and 2 Thessalonians 1:9–10?

Now we will consider a different but related set of passages. These passages express the human desire for God to be glorified and worshipped.

PSALM 57:9–11

> [9] I will give thanks to you, O Lord, among the peoples; I will sing praises to you among the nations. [10] For your steadfast love is great to the heavens, your faithfulness to the clouds.

¹¹ Be exalted, O God, above the heavens! Let your glory be over all the earth!

PSALM 96:1–9

¹ Oh sing to the LORD a new song; sing to the LORD, all the earth! ² Sing to the LORD, bless his name; tell of his salvation from day to day. ³ Declare his glory among the nations, his marvelous works among all the peoples! ⁴ For great is the LORD, and greatly to be praised; he is to be feared above all gods. ⁵ For all the gods of the peoples are worthless idols, but the LORD made the heavens. ⁶ Splendor and majesty are before him; strength and beauty are in his sanctuary. ⁷ Ascribe to the LORD, O families of the peoples, ascribe to the LORD glory and strength! ⁸ Ascribe to the LORD the glory due his name; bring an offering, and come into his courts! ⁹ Worship the LORD in the splendor of holiness; tremble before him, all the earth!

*QUESTION 6: How do these two passages from the Psalms relate to Isaiah 48:9–11? (Review your answer to Question 4.) How does God's passion for his glory relate to our passion for his glory?

DAY 4: GOD-CENTERED VS. SELF-CENTERED

If you have ever been exposed to the teaching ministry of John Piper before, you will know that one of his favorite hyphenated words is "God-centered." He is constantly emphasizing that we must be God-centered because God is God-centered.

*QUESTION 7: What do you think that the word *God-centered* means? Define this term using your own words.

QUESTION 8: What's the alternative to being God-centered? Why is it that more people are not God-centered?

In the previous lesson, we read Ephesians 5:18–21.

EPHESIANS 5:18–21

> [18] And do not get drunk with wine, for that is debauchery, but be filled with the Spirit, [19] addressing one another in psalms and hymns and spiritual songs, singing and making melody to the Lord with your heart, [20] giving thanks always and for everything to God the Father in the name of our Lord Jesus Christ, [21] submitting to one another out of reverence for Christ.

Here are some of Piper's comments on what the phrase "to the Lord" (in verse 19) means:

> "To the Lord" means that worship is to be God-centered. . . . But not just God-centered in that everything in worship relates to God, but also God-centered in that

everything in worship is done toward God—in the presence of God, with a view to God's hearing it and seeing it, with a desire that God receive it into his hearing with approval and delight.[3]

DAY 5: IS GOD LOVING TO EXALT HIMSELF?

Our study in this lesson thus far raises a crucial question: If God's central passion is to pursue his own glory, then how can it be that God loves us? Or, if God is so focused on glorifying himself, then don't we get lost in the picture?

Every Christian knows John 3:16. But compare this verse with three other verses in the Gospel of John.

JOHN 3:16–17

[16] For God so loved the world, that he gave his only Son, that whoever believes in him should not perish but have eternal life. [17] For God did not send his Son into the world to condemn the world, but in order that the world might be saved through him.

JOHN 5:36

The works that the Father has given me to accomplish, the very works that I am doing, bear witness about me that the Father has sent me.

JOHN 17:4

I glorified you on earth, having accomplished the work that you gave me to do.

QUESTION 9: How is John 3:16–17 related to John 5:36 and 17:4? Did God send his Son into the world for our salvation or for his glory? Is God's gift of Jesus an expression of his love for us or his desire to glorify himself?

If by our worship we glorify God, is God loving to command us to worship him? Is God loving toward us to exalt himself? C. S. Lewis has an insight that helps us answer these troubling questions.

The most obvious fact about praise . . . strangely escaped me. . . . I had never noticed that all enjoyment spontaneously overflows into praise. . . . The world rings with praise—lovers praising their mistresses, readers their favorite poet, walkers praising the countryside, players praising their favorite game—praise of weather, wines, dishes, actors, horses, colleges, countries, historical personages, children, flowers, mountains, rare stamps, rare beetles, even sometimes politicians and scholars. . . . My whole, more general difficulty about praise of God depended on my absurdly denying to us, as regards the supremely Valuable, what we delight to do, what indeed we can't help doing, about everything else we value.

I think we delight to praise what we enjoy because the praise not merely expresses but completes the enjoyment; it is its appointed consummation. It is not out of compliment that lovers keep on telling one another how beautiful they are, the delight is incomplete till it is expressed.[4]

*QUESTION 10: How does the insight that praise is the appointed consummation of joy address the question of how God is loving to command our praise?

FURTHER UP AND FURTHER IN

John Piper, like C. S. Lewis, often teaches the truth of God's Word with vivid metaphors. You will find one such metaphor in the following article.

Read John Piper, "Two Ways to Be Silent before Majesty," an online sermon at the Desiring God Web site.

QUESTION 11: How does a climber "honor" the eastern face of Mount Everest?

QUESTION 12: If God is like the eastern face of Mount Everest, would it be loving for him to call people to the silence of beauty instead of allowing them to remain in the silence of blindness? Explain your answer.

Read John Piper, *Desiring God,* pages 44–49.[5]

QUESTION 13: According to Piper, what are two reasons why people stumble over the truth that God exalts himself and seeks the praise of men? How does Piper respond to each objection?

QUESTION 14: Why is it not enough for God to only give us himself? Why must he also pursue praise from us?

QUESTION 15: Record at least one lingering question about what you've been studying that you could share with the group during the next group session.

WHILE YOU WATCH THE DVD, TAKE NOTES

Question: What is the inward essence of worship?

Thesis: The essential, vital, indispensable, defining heart of worship is the experience of being _____ with God. This _____ in God magnifies God in the heart. This explains why the apostle Paul makes so little distinction between _____ as a congregational service and _____ as a pattern of daily life.

Question: Is this biblical?

"The root of our passion and thirst for _____ is God's own infinite exuberance for _____."

Summary: "God's overflowing joy in his own _____ is the root and basis of ours. God is so exuberant about his _____ that he makes its display the goal of all he does. Therefore, so should we."

Question: Why is it a loving thing for God to be so self-exalting?

Quotation from C. S. Lewis

AFTER YOU WATCH THE DVD, DISCUSS WHAT YOU'VE LEARNED

1) Is it a comfort to you to know that in everything God does, he has the goal of displaying his own infinite worth?

2) Imagine that you are in a conversation with unbelieving friends of yours. They hear that the Bible teaches that God does everything for his own glory and they think that is extremely vain of God. How would you explain to them to God is not vain but *loving* to pursue his own glory?

3) Has it become any clearer to you why John Piper is devoting so much time in this seminar to defining what worship is? Could someone form a philosophy of corporate worship without carefully defining what worship is?

AFTER YOU DISCUSS, MAKE APPLICATION

1) What was the most meaningful part of this lesson for you? Was there a sentence, concept, or idea that really struck you? Why? Record your thoughts in the space below.

2) Compose a prayer that praises God for who he is, that asks God to glorify himself, and that thanks God for loving you by showing you his glory. Incorporate in your prayer some of what you have learned from this lesson.

NOTES

1. This excerpt is taken from the *Gravity and Gladness* seminar notes.
2. John Piper, "Worship God!" an online sermon at the Desiring God Web site.
3. John Piper, "Singing and Making Melody to the Lord," an online sermon at the Desiring God Web site.
4. C. S. Lewis, *Reflections on the Psalms*, as quoted by John Piper in the *Gravity and Gladness* seminar notes.
5. John Piper's book *Desiring God* (rev. ed.; Sisters, OR: Multnomah, 2003) is available online for viewing or download at the Desiring God Web site.

LESSON 6
LEWIS AND PROWSE ON WORSHIP
A Companion Study to Gravity and Gladness, *Session 5*

LESSON OBJECTIVES
It is our prayer that after you have finished this lesson . . .

> You will have reviewed what you have learned through this study guide thus far.

> You will begin to think about what the tone of worship services should be.

> You will be able to address an objection to the God-centeredness of God.

BEFORE YOU WATCH THE DVD, STUDY AND PREPARE

DAY 1: A BIT OF REVIEW
It might be helpful at this point to include a bit of review. Please remember that the topic for the seminar and this study guide is corporate worship. We are interested in forming an understanding of what corporate worship should be on Sunday mornings (or at

other times). The first and most important step in this process is to understand what worship *is*. If we don't know what worship is, then how can we know that we're actually worshipping when we come together? And how can we design and participate in worship services if we are ignorant as to what worship is? Thus, roughly the first half (!) of this study guide is devoted to defining what worship is, while the second half reflects on how we can promote worship in corporate services.

QUESTION 1: Without turning back to previous lessons, summarize what you've learned about worship thus far. What are some of the key insights that you've gained?

*QUESTION 2: What questions do you have about corporate worship services that you hope will be addressed in the rest of this course?

DAY 2: ISAIAH 34 IN WORSHIP

In subsequent lessons we will discuss what the tone or "feel" of corporate worship services should be. We anticipate that discussion in this day's study and the next.

Worship of God feeds on a vision of God. This is what it means to worship "in truth" (John 4:24). The following passage is one account of what God is like.

Slowly read Isaiah 34:1–7.

ISAIAH 34:1–7

[1] Draw near, O nations, to hear, and give attention, O peoples! Let the earth hear, and all that fills it; the world, and all that comes from it. [2] For the LORD is enraged against all the nations, and furious against all their host; he has devoted them to destruction, has given them over for slaughter. [3] Their slain shall be cast out, and the stench of their corpses shall rise; the mountains shall flow with their blood. [4] All the host of heaven shall rot away, and the skies roll up like a scroll. All their host shall fall, as leaves fall from the vine, like leaves falling from the fig tree. [5] For my sword has drunk its fill in the heavens; behold, it descends for judgment upon Edom, upon the people I have devoted to destruction. [6] The LORD has a sword; it is sated with blood; it is gorged with fat, with the blood of lambs and goats, with the fat of the kidneys of rams. For the LORD has a sacrifice in Bozrah, a great slaughter in the land of Edom. [7] Wild oxen shall fall with them, and young steers with the mighty bulls. Their land shall drink its fill of blood, and their soil shall be gorged with fat.

QUESTION 3: As you read this passage, what emotions are stirred up within your heart? Why might this passage have been included in the Bible? What effect is it designed to have on those who read it?

*QUESTION 4: Does a passage like Isaiah 34 belong in a corporate worship service? If not, why not? If so, then what would be missing if a passage like this was never included in corporate worship services? What tone would a passage like this set in corporate worship?

[Careless worship] comes from the failure to feel the greatness of God's sovereign love and the greatness of his majestic fatherhood.

It is greatness in particular that is crucial when worship is at stake. You might have a horse like Flicka, or Fury, or Black Beauty, or a dog like Rin Tin Tin, or Lassie, or Benji that saves your life a hundred times. You might have a deep affection for the animal and weep when it dies. But you are never tempted to bow down and worship it. The same is true of a human friend. The closest bond of friendship and love and unity might develop, but you never think of worshiping your friend. Why? Because one indispensable element in worship is GREATNESS, majesty, grandeur. So when careless worship is the issue, God focuses attention not first on the gentleness of his love or the tenderness of his fatherhood, but on the sovereign freedom of his love and the majesty of his fatherhood.[1]

DAY 3: ISAIAH 35 IN WORSHIP

The heavy and dark chapter of Isaiah 34 is followed by a much different chapter—Isaiah 35. Read the beginning and end of this chapter, while you keep Isaiah 34 in mind.

ISAIAH 35:1–2, 8–10

[1] The wilderness and the dry land shall be glad; the desert shall rejoice and blossom like the crocus; [2] it shall blossom abundantly and rejoice with joy and singing. The glory of Lebanon shall be given to it, the majesty of Carmel and Sharon. They shall see the glory of the LORD, the majesty of our God. . . . [8] And a highway shall be there, and it shall be called the Way of Holiness; the unclean shall not pass over it. It shall belong to those who walk on the way; even if they are fools, they shall not go astray. [9] No lion shall be there, nor shall any ravenous beast come up on it; they shall not be found there, but the redeemed shall walk there. [10] And the ransomed of the LORD shall return and come to Zion with singing; everlasting joy shall be upon their heads; they shall obtain gladness and joy, and sorrow and sighing shall flee away.

QUESTION 5: As you read *this* passage, what emotions are stirred up within your heart? Why might this passage have been included in the Bible? What effect is it designed to have on those who read it?

*QUESTION 6: Is it possible to present the truths of both Isaiah 34 and Isaiah 35 *together* in Christian corporate worship services? What are the dangers of a service that concentrates solely on only one chapter of these two?

DAY 4: ANSWERING MICHAEL PROWSE

At the end of the previous lesson we raised a possible objection to what we've asserted about God's pursuit of his own glory. Some might hear this and say, "How vain of God! What kind of egocentric God would demand that people worship him?"

This objection is stated well by Michael Prowse, who wrote the following in 2003 in the London *Financial Times*:

> Worship is an aspect of religion that I always found difficult to understand. Suppose we postulate an omnipotent being who, for reasons inscrutable to us, decided to create something other than himself. Why should he . . . expect us to worship him? We didn't ask to be created. Our lives are often troubled. We know that human tyrants, puffed up with pride, crave adulation and homage. But a morally perfect God would surely have no character defects. So why are all those people on their knees every Sunday?[2]

*QUESTION 7: Restate Michael Prowse's objection to God's demand for worship in your own words.

QUESTION 8: How would you respond to Michael Prowse? Compose a short paragraph that answers his objection.

DAY 5: RETURNING TO C. S. LEWIS

We will now look once again at the quotation from C. S. Lewis that was so formative for John Piper:

> The most obvious fact about praise . . . strangely escaped me. . . . I had never noticed that all enjoyment spontaneously overflows into praise. . . . The world rings with praise—lovers praising their mistresses, readers their favorite poet, walkers praising the countryside, players praising their favorite game—praise of weather, wines, dishes, actors, horses, colleges, countries, historical personages, children, flowers, mountains, rare stamps, rare beetles, even sometimes politicians and scholars. . . . My whole, more general difficulty about praise of God depended on my absurdly denying to us, as regards the supremely Valuable, what we delight to do, what indeed we can't help doing, about everything else we value.
>
> I think we delight to praise what we enjoy because the praise not merely expresses but completes the enjoyment; it is its appointed consummation. It is not out of compliment that lovers keep on telling one another how beautiful they are, the delight is incomplete till it is expressed.[3]

*QUESTION 9: Why is Lewis's insight so important? In other words, what problem or objection does his insight answer?

Lewis writes, "I think we delight to praise what we enjoy because the praise not merely expresses but completes the enjoyment; it is its appointed consummation."

QUESTION 10: Can you think of an everyday example that would illustrate this point? Lewis mentions the delight lovers experience in telling each other how beautiful they are. Can you think of another such example? Record it below.

FURTHER UP AND FURTHER IN

In this lesson we have already encountered Michael Prowse's objection to God's demand for worship. We will now read an open letter that John Piper wrote in response to Michael Prowse. Understanding the reasons why God demands our praise is crucially important in planning, leading, and participating in corporate worship services.

Read John Piper, "An Open Letter to Michael Prowse," an online article at the Desiring God Web site.

QUESTION 11: If you had to choose one sentence in this letter that summarized John Piper's response to Michael Prowse, which sentence would you choose and why?

QUESTION 12: How does John's Piper's response compare to your own? (Review your answer to Question 8, if necessary.) What have you learned in reading this article?

Read or listen to John Piper, "The Curse of Careless Worship," **an online sermon at the Desiring God Web site.**

QUESTION 13: According to Piper, what is the origin and essence of careless worship? Put Piper's answer into your own words.

QUESTION 14: What are the three dead-end streets that Piper mentions with regard to excellence in worship? Have you been down any of these dead-end streets in corporate worship before? If so, describe your experience.

QUESTION 15: What are two specific things that you can do in order to combat careless worship in your own life? Record your ideas below.

WHILE YOU WATCH THE DVD, TAKE NOTES

Opening Prayer and Morning Devotions

Gravity (Isaiah 34:2; John 3:36)

Gladness (Isaiah 35)

Review

How is God loving to pursue his glory?

New Yorker illustration

Red Skelton illustration

"When God commands you to praise that which is infinitely praiseworthy, he's doing it for _____ sake as well as _____ sake, because your praising that which is most beautiful, most satisfying, is not some kind of demanded tack-on—it's the completion, it's the consummation—God wants the fullness of your _____ and the fullness of your _____ can only be found in him."

AFTER YOU WATCH THE DVD, DISCUSS WHAT YOU'VE LEARNED

1) Piper refers to Isaiah 34 and Isaiah 35 as examples of gravity and gladness in worship. Can you think of other chapters or verses in the Bible that reflect the realities of gravity and gladness in worship?

2) Piper gives two illustrations in this session of delight being incomplete until it is expressed in praise—the illustrations of the *New Yorker* cartoons and Red Skelton comedy monologues. Can you think of an illustration from your own life experience that makes the same point?

3) How has Piper's teaching about God's pursuit of his own glory and praise changed the way in which you think about corporate worship?

AFTER YOU DISCUSS, MAKE APPLICATION

1) What was the most meaningful part of this lesson for you? Was there a sentence, concept, or idea that really struck you? Why? Record your thoughts in the space below.

2) Imagine that someone has written an editorial in your local newspaper mocking the God of the Bible as ego-centric and emotionally insecure. Write a brief response to this editorial, defending God's demand for praise. Keep in mind your audience, and incorporate some of what you have learned in this lesson.

NOTES

1. John Piper, "The Curse of Careless Worship," an online sermon at the Desiring God Web site.
2. Michael Prowse as quoted by John Piper, "An Open Letter to Michael Prowse," an online article at the Desiring God Web site.
3. C. S. Lewis, *Reflections on the Psalms*, as quoted by John Piper in the *Gravity and Gladness* seminar notes.

LESSON 7
THE LOVING DEMAND FOR WORSHIP
A Companion Study to Gravity and Gladness, *Session 6*

LESSON OBJECTIVES

It is our prayer that after you have finished this lesson . . .

> › You will be able to defend the idea that God's demand for worship is loving.

> › You will perceive the connection between truth and affections.

> › You will be able to explain how godly sorrow relates to joy.

BEFORE YOU WATCH THE DVD, STUDY AND PREPARE

DAY 1: A PRIESTLY PRAYER OF LOVE?

In the previous two lessons we've learned from C. S. Lewis that God is loving to command us to praise him. This is because praise is simply the appointed consummation of joy. While Lewis argued for these things from experience and reason, we will now consider

84

a biblical passage that supports the idea that God's pursuit of his own glory is also love toward his people.

Jesus' prayer in John 17 is often called "the High-Priestly Prayer." But is Jesus' prayer for us or for himself? Compare the following verses:

JOHN 17:1, 4–5

[1] When Jesus had spoken these words, he lifted up his eyes to heaven, and said, "Father, the hour has come; glorify your Son that the Son may glorify you. . . . [4] I glorified you on earth, having accomplished the work that you gave me to do. [5] And now, Father, glorify me in your own presence with the glory that I had with you before the world existed."

JOHN 17:9, 20

[9] I am praying for them. I am not praying for the world but for those whom you have given me, for they are yours. . . . [20] I do not ask for these only, but also for those who will believe in me through their word.

*QUESTION 1: Is Jesus' prayer for his own glory or for the good of his disciples? Explain.

Skim the entire prayer in John 17.

QUESTION 2: Can you find any evidence in John 17 that Jesus' prayer to be glorified is a loving thing to pray for his disciples? If so, record it below and explain why it counts as evidence.

DAY 2: A PARAGRAPH FROM JONATHAN EDWARDS

If worship of God is intended to glorify God, then we must know how God is glorified in order to worship him properly. The following paragraph (separated into two quotations) from Jonathan Edwards helps us to continue thinking about the nature of true worship.

> God glorifies Himself toward the creatures also in two ways: 1. By appearing to . . . their understanding. 2. In communicating Himself to their hearts, and in their rejoicing and delighting in, and enjoying, the manifestations which He makes of Himself . . . God is glorified not only by His glory's being seen, but by its being rejoiced in. When those that see it delight in it, God is more glorified than if they only see it.[1]

QUESTION 3: According to these sentences, how does God glorify himself "toward the creatures"?

The paragraph continues,

> His glory is then received by the whole soul, both by the understanding and by the heart. God made the world that He might communicate, and the creature receive, His glory; and that it might [be] received both by the mind and heart. He that testifies his idea of God's glory [doesn't] glorify God so much as he that testifies also his approbation of it and his delight in it.[2]

*QUESTION 4: Why is it important to touch both the head and the heart in corporate worship?

DAY 3: MORE FROM JONATHAN EDWARDS

Jonathan Edwards had this to say about his responsibility as a preacher:

> I should think myself in the way of my duty, to raise the affections of my hearers as high as I possibly can, provided they are affected with nothing but truth, and with affections that are not disagreeable to the nature of what they are affected with.[3]

*QUESTION 5: In the quotation above, Jonathan Edwards provides two qualifications to his initial statement that it is his duty "to raise the affections of my hearers as high as I possibly can." Underline these two qualifications. Why are these qualifications so important?

QUESTION 6: Review the quotations from Jonathan Edwards that have been reproduced in this lesson thus far. How might the truths expressed in these quotations affect a church's philosophy of corporate worship?

Here is a statement from the Bethlehem Baptist Church Web site about the mind and the heart:

> We are convinced that truth really matters and that right belief is essential for sustained, persevering right living and affections. And we want to keep these two in proper order. Right belief is not our ultimate goal. Rather, we aim deeper; we aim for the heart. We want to help you in your quest for joy. In Pastor John Piper's words, "From a biblical standpoint studying and thinking and knowing are never ends in themselves; they always stand in the service of feeling and willing and doing. The mind is the servant of the heart. Knowledge exists for the sake of love. And all theology worth its salt produces doxology."[4]

DAY 4: REJOICE!

The book of Psalms was Israel's songbook. It not only *expressed* their praise to God, but it also *called for* praise.

Listed below are several texts from the book of Psalms. As you read them, underline every command.

PSALM 5:11

> But let all who take refuge in you rejoice; let them ever sing for joy, and spread your protection over them, that those who love your name may exult in you.

PSALM 32:11

> Be glad in the LORD, and rejoice, O righteous, and shout for joy, all you upright in heart!

PSALM 35:27

> Let those who delight in my righteousness shout for joy and be glad and say evermore, "Great is the LORD, who delights in the welfare of his servant!"

PSALM 37:4

> Delight yourself in the LORD, and he will give you the desires of your heart.

PSALM 40:16

> But may all who seek you rejoice and be glad in you; may those who love your salvation say continually, "Great is the LORD!"

PSALM 70:4

> May all who seek you rejoice and be glad in you! May those who love your salvation say evermore, "God is great!"

PSALM 97:1

The LORD reigns, let the earth rejoice; let the many coastlands be glad!

PSALM 100:2

Serve the LORD with gladness! Come into his presence with singing!

PSALM 105:3

Glory in his holy name; let the hearts of those who seek the LORD rejoice!

PSALM 149:2

Let Israel be glad in his Maker; let the children of Zion rejoice in their King!

QUESTION 7: When God calls for us to rejoice in him he is . . .

a. loving us.

b. honoring himself.

c. being selfish.

d. being indifferent to his own glory.

The book of Psalms, as well as the entire Old Testament, is filled with commands for us to be happy. We see this same phenomenon in the New Testament.

As you read the following texts, underline every instance in which joy is commanded.

MATTHEW 5:11–12

11 Blessed are you when others revile you and persecute you and utter all kinds of evil against you falsely on my account. 12 Rejoice and be glad, for your reward is great in heaven, for so they persecuted the prophets who were before you.

LUKE 10:20

Nevertheless, do not rejoice in this, that the spirits are subject to you, but rejoice that your names are written in heaven.

ROMANS 12:12

Rejoice in hope, be patient in tribulation, be constant in prayer.

2 CORINTHIANS 13:11

Finally, brothers, rejoice. Aim for restoration, comfort one another, agree with one another, live in peace; and the God of love and peace will be with you.

PHILIPPIANS 4:4

Rejoice in the Lord always; again I will say, Rejoice.

1 THESSALONIANS 5:16–18

16 Rejoice always, 17 pray without ceasing, 18 give thanks in all circumstances; for this is the will of God in Christ Jesus for you.

1 PETER 4:13

> But rejoice insofar as you share Christ's sufferings, that you may also rejoice and be glad when his glory is revealed.

*QUESTION 8: Is it possible to command the emotions? And why would God be interested in *demanding* our happiness?

MATTHEW 2:1–2, 9–11

> [1] Now after Jesus was born in Bethlehem of Judea in the days of Herod the king, behold, wise men from the east came to Jerusalem, [2] saying, "Where is he who has been born king of the Jews? For we saw his star when it rose and have come to worship him." . . . [9] After listening to the king, they went on their way. And behold, the star that they had seen when it rose went before them until it came to rest over the place where the child was. [10] When they saw the star, they rejoiced exceedingly with great joy. [11] And going into the house they saw the child with Mary his mother, and they fell down and worshiped him. Then, opening their treasures, they offered him gifts, gold and frankincense and myrrh.

In commenting on verse 10 ("When they saw the star, they rejoiced exceedingly with great joy"), Piper says the following:

> Now this is a quadruple way of saying they rejoiced. It would have been much to say they rejoiced. More to say they rejoiced with joy. More to say they rejoiced with great joy. And even more to say they rejoiced exceedingly with great joy. And what was all this joy about?—they were on

their way to the Messiah. They were almost there. I cannot avoid the impression then that true worship is not just ascribing authority and dignity to Christ; it is doing this joyfully. It is doing it because you have come to see something about Christ that is so desirable that being near him to ascribe authority and dignity to him personally is overwhelmingly compelling.[5]

DAY 5: CAN WEEPING BE WORSHIP?

We've asserted thus far that the essence of true worship is satisfaction or joy in God. Does this mean that there is no place for crying, godly sorrow, or brokenness in corporate worship services?

Remember that Paul commanded the Romans to "rejoice with those who rejoice, weep with those who weep" (Romans 12:15). Is rejoicing at all related to weeping? Read the following thoughts on this question from John Piper:

Christian joy reveals itself as dissatisfied contentment whenever it perceives human need. It starts to expand in love to fill that need and bring about the joy of faith in the heart of the other person. But since there is often a time lapse between our perception of a person's need and our eventual rejoicing in the person's restored joy, there is a place for weeping in that interval. The weeping of compassion is the weeping of joy impeded in the extension of itself to another.[6]

QUESTION 9: Summarize this quotation in your own words. According to Piper, how is weeping related to joy?

*QUESTION 10: The quotation above relates weeping to love that one human might have for another. How would Piper's idea relate to weeping out of love for God? How would this bring glory to God?

PSALM 51:7–12

> [7] Purge me with hyssop, and I shall be clean; wash me, and I shall be whiter than snow. [8] Let me hear joy and gladness; let the bones that you have broken rejoice. [9] Hide your face from my sins, and blot out all my iniquities. [10] Create in me a clean heart, O God, and renew a right spirit within me. [11] Cast me not away from your presence, and take not your Holy Spirit from me. [12] Restore to me the joy of your salvation, and uphold me with a willing spirit.

For more reflection on this issue, see the "Further Up and Further In" section that follows.

FURTHER UP AND FURTHER IN

We have seen in this lesson that God commands our happiness.

> The number one duty of worship is not merely a duty to perform outward acts. It is a duty to feel inward affections. It is a duty the way C. S. Lewis spoke of it in a letter to Sheldon Vanauken when he said, "It is a Christian duty, as you know, for every one to be as happy as he can."

Or the way Jeremy Taylor spoke of it when he said, "God threatens terrible things, if we will not be happy."

Or as the psalmist commands us, "Delight thyself in the Lord!"[7]

QUESTION 11: Rewrite Lewis's or Taylor's quote in your own words.

God also demands other emotions in worship.

PSALM 103:1–5

Of David. [1] Bless the LORD, O my soul, and all that is within me, bless his holy name! [2] Bless the LORD, O my soul, and forget not all his benefits, [3] who forgives all your iniquity, who heals all your diseases, [4] who redeems your life from the pit, who crowns you with steadfast love and mercy, [5] who satisfies you with good so that your youth is renewed like the eagle's.

There is always a sense of shortfall between our spiritual perception of the greatness of God and our spiritual affection in worshiping God. The intensity of the heart never seems up to what his glory deserves.

That's why one of the most common impulses of genuine worship is to plead with your own soul: "Bless the Lord, O my soul!" Come on, soul, where are you? Why do you sleep before this God? Why are you dull and sluggish? Wake up! Look at what God has done! Look at what he is like! . . .

But the very recognition of this shortcoming is worship—our sense of discontent that our soul isn't fully kicking in signals how great the worth of God really is. Otherwise we wouldn't be pressing for a deeper response. And crying out against the shortcoming of our soul, like David does, is even more worship. "Bless the Lord, O my soul; and all that is within me—not just some of me, not just half my heart, not just half my energy, not just half my mind, but all that is within me—bless his holy name."[8]

QUESTION 12: How might discontentment, godly sorrow, or regret honor God?

Read John Piper, *Desiring God,* **pages 96–97.**[9]

QUESTION 13: What three stages of worship does Piper describe? How is God glorified in each stage?

QUESTION 14: Why is it important to teach about all three stages of worship? In other words, what might be lost if teaching on worship only mentioned one of these stages?

QUESTION 15: How might an understanding of these three stages affect the planning and leading of corporate worship services? How could a congregation be unified in worship if there were people in each of these three stages on a Sunday morning?

WHILE YOU WATCH THE DVD, TAKE NOTES

"So what I'm doing now . . . is . . . to show you that *biblically* God's pursuit of his own _____ is _____."

John 17:1–5, 24–26

"Love labors, at great cost to itself, in order to bring the beloved into the fullest and longest _____ with what is infinitely _____, forever. That's the definition of what love does. And that's what God does when he pursues our enjoyment of his _____."

Jonathan Edwards

Truth and affections

Commands to rejoice

What about godly sorrow?

AFTER YOU WATCH THE DVD, DISCUSS WHAT YOU'VE LEARNED

1) How does Piper's teaching about love (and God's love) compare to what the world would say about love (and God's love)?

2) In your opinion, do most evangelical churches focus more on the head or the heart in corporate worship services? Give examples to defend your opinion. What could be done to bring more balance in worship between truth and affections?

3) Why might Piper have decided to ask and answer the question about godly sorrow? What might have been lost in the seminar if Piper had not addressed this issue?

AFTER YOU DISCUSS, MAKE APPLICATION

1) What was the most meaningful part of this lesson for you? Was there a sentence, concept, or idea that really struck you? Why? Record your thoughts in the space below.

2) Design a Sunday school lesson for middle-school students. The lesson could either stress the importance of both truth and affections in the worship of God or teach how God can be glorified in our sorrow over sin. Make your teaching age appropriate, and incorporate what you've learned from this lesson.

NOTES

1. Jonathan Edwards, as quoted by John Piper in the *Gravity and Gladness* seminar notes (which can be found at the Desiring God Web site).
2. Ibid.
3. Jonathan Edwards, as quoted by John Piper in *Desiring God*, 103, available for viewing or download online at the Desiring God Web site.
4. This excerpt was taken from http://www.hopeingod.org/about-us/who-we-are/our-beliefs.
5. John Piper, "We Have Come to Worship Him," an online sermon at the Desiring God Web site.
6. John Piper's book *Desiring God*, 124–125, available for viewing or download online at the Desiring God Web site.
7. John Piper, "You Shall Worship the Lord Your God," an online sermon at the Desiring God Web site.
8. John Piper, "Forget Not All His Benefits," an online sermon at the Desiring God Web site.
9. John Piper's book *Desiring God*, available for viewing or download online at the Desiring God Web site.

LESSON 8
SOME IMPLICATIONS FOR CORPORATE WORSHIP
A Companion Study to Gravity and Gladness, *Session 7*

LESSON OBJECTIVES

It is our prayer that after you have finished this lesson . . .

> You will be able to restate Piper's four implications for corporate worship.

> You will understand the meaning and significance of the phrase "undistracting excellence" in the context of corporate worship.

> You will identify the purpose of corporate worship.

BEFORE YOU WATCH THE DVD, STUDY AND PREPARE

DAY 1: IMMANUEL KANT AND SUNDAY MORNINGS

This lesson and the ones that follow will build on the biblical foundation that has already been laid in previous lessons. We have seen that the essential, vital, indispensable, defining heart of worship is the experience of being satisfied in God. And the reason satisfaction in God is the heart of worship is that God is most glorified in us when we are most satisfied in him. This lesson will draw out some implications of these truths for corporate worship.

Examine these two quotations made about Immanuel Kant.

"If there lurks in most modern minds the notion that to desire our own good and earnestly to hope for the enjoyment of it is a bad thing, I submit that this notion has crept in from Kant and the Stoics."

"An action is moral, said Kant, only if one has no desire to perform it, but performs it out of a sense of duty and derives no benefit from it of any sort, neither material nor spiritual. A benefit destroys the moral value of an action."[1]

QUESTION 1: Based on the work you've done in this course thus far, would you agree with Kant? Must worship of God not be motivated by the pleasure we might derive from it? Explain your answer.

*QUESTION 2: In your opinion, how prevalent is Kant's ethic (as represented above) in Christian churches today? How does this way of thinking manifest itself in corporate worship services?

DAY 2: DO WE GIVE OR RECEIVE ON SUNDAY MORNINGS?

The title of this day's study is an important and fundamental question to ask. Our answer to it will shape our philosophy of worship in a thousand ways, both consciously and unconsciously.

Examine the following statement, which is typical of what many pastors say about the problem of corporate worship in their churches:

> "The problem is that our people don't come on Sunday morning to give; they only come to get. If they came to give, we would have life in our services."[2]

*QUESTION 3: Have you ever heard a variation of this sentiment? If so, record it below. If not, create another statement, like the one above, that arises from the mind-set that people should come to give on Sunday mornings.

QUESTION 4: How would you evaluate or respond to the statement constructed by John Piper above? How would you evaluate or respond to the statement you wrote down as your answer to Question 3?

> God is magnified when we cherish him as gain above all things, and come to him to tell him that and to find more of him. God serves us by giving life and breath and everything about himself that goes to the deepest recesses of our hearts. We worship first and foremost by thirsting and hungering after God above all things. And that means that we worship first and foremost by being served by God. It is a worship service, because the service starts with God's serving us what we so desperately need, namely, himself.[3]

DAY 3: WHAT IS AT THE CENTER OF OUR WORSHIP?

We're assuming that most Christian pastors and worship leaders would say that their aim is to make God the center of corporate worship. But it might also be safe to say that there is not as much reflection as there should be about *how* to make God the center of worship. Substitutes for God can easily and subtly creep in and become the real focus and center of attention in corporate worship.

*QUESTION 5: Brainstorm a list of five things that can intentionally or unintentionally replace God as the focus of corporate worship. Record these things below.

    1.

    2.

    3.

    4.

    5.

QUESTION 6: Choose one thing that can replace God as the center of attention out of the five things you've listed in Question 5. If this one thing became the functional center of corporate worship, then how might church leaders begin to measure the power and excellence of the worship services?

DAY 4: IS WORSHIP A MEANS OR AN END?

Your study thus far flows nicely into this next question: Is worship a means to something else or an end in itself?

*QUESTION 7: Pretend that you are asked to present on this question at a church meeting. Setting aside your own convictions for a moment, construct the best arguments you can think of for both sides of the question. In other words, write down a sketch of how you would argue for the idea that worship is a means to something else. Then write down your arguments for the idea that worship is an end in itself.

QUESTION 8: Which of the arguments you wrote down in Question 7 do you find the most compelling? Explain.

DAY 5: SUNDAY MORNINGS AND THE REST OF LIFE

This last day's study brings us back to some of what we've learned in a previous lesson.

Review your answers and notes to Lesson 4, "The Boycott of 'Worship.'"

*QUESTION 9: In view of the work you've already done, would you say that all of life is worship or not? Defend your answer.

In the video session corresponding to this lesson, John Piper will assert, "All Christian behavior is to be done out of satisfaction in God and with a view to preserving and increasing our satisfaction in God." He then attempts to support this assertion with the following biblical verse:

LUKE 12:33

Sell your possessions, and give to the needy. Provide yourselves with moneybags that do not grow old, with a treasure in the heavens that does not fail, where no thief approaches and no moth destroys.

QUESTION 10: Do you think that Luke 12:33 supports Piper's assertion? (Notice also Luke 14:13–14 below.) If so, explain how. If not, explain why not.

LUKE 14:13–14

13 But when you give a feast, invite the poor, the crippled, the lame, the blind, 14 and you will be blessed, because they cannot repay you. For you will be repaid at the resurrection of the just.

FURTHER UP AND FURTHER IN

Read or listen to John Piper, "Worship Is an End in Itself," an online sermon at the Desiring God Web site.

Consider Jesus' devastating critique of the Pharisees.

MATTHEW 15:7–9

7 You hypocrites! Well did Isaiah prophesy of you, when he said: 8 "This people honors me with their lips, but their heart is far from me; 9 in vain do they worship me, teaching as doctrines the commandments of men."

QUESTION 11: What does Piper say about these verses? Record his insights below. (If you answered Questions 11 and 12 in Lesson 4, compare Piper's insights to your own.)

QUESTION 12: According to Piper, what is the danger for most evangelicals, if not emotionalism?

QUESTION 13: List the feelings that Piper mentions as examples of emotions that turn outward acts into genuine worship. Of those that you list, which feeling toward God do you most often experience? Which feeling do you experience the least often?

Worship is an end in itself, and we worship God by receiving from him everything we need so that he is glorified as the self-sufficient and powerful one.

The Bible is concerned to call us back from idolatry to serve the true and living God (1 Thess. 1:9). But it is also concerned to keep us from serving the true God in the wrong way. There is a way to serve God that belittles and dishonors Him. Therefore, we must take heed lest we recruit servants whose labor diminishes the glory of the All-powerful Provider. If Jesus said that He came *not* to be served, service may be rebellion.[4]

Christians who are truly worshiping God in corporate services are both receiving and giving. But there are ways in which to belittle and dishonor God by how we serve and by what we are hoping to receive.

QUESTION 14: What is the right way to glorify God in giving? What is the right way to glorify God in receiving? What is the wrong way to glorify in giving? What is the wrong way to glorify God in receiving?

QUESTION 15: Why do you think that corporate gatherings of Christians on Sunday morning are often called "worship *services*"? (Consult your answer to Question 3 of Lesson 4.) Is this term a helpful one in your mind? If so, why? If not, what would you propose as an alternative?

WHILE YOU WATCH THE DVD, TAKE NOTES

The essence of worship is being satisfied in God: What are the implications of that?

Implication #1: The pursuit of joy in God is not _____. It is our highest duty.

Implication #2: Worship becomes radically _____. "Undistracting excellence."

Implication #3: Worship is an _____ in itself.

Implication #4: All of _____ is an expression of worship.

AFTER YOU WATCH THE DVD, DISCUSS WHAT YOU'VE LEARNED

1) In your opinion, is your church's worship service God centered? How do you know?

2) Discuss the phrase "undistracting excellence." What does Piper mean by this phrase? Why are both words in this phrase important? How might a church's worship service change if it adopted a commitment to undistracting excellence?

3) Why does John Piper in this seminar about corporate worship on Sunday mornings stress repeatedly that all of life is worship? Doesn't this emphasis undermine his focus on corporate worship?

AFTER YOU DISCUSS, MAKE APPLICATION

1) What was the most meaningful part of this lesson for you? Was there a sentence, concept, or idea that really struck you? Why? Record your thoughts in the space below.

2) Suppose that a friend of yours is moving to a new area and is looking for a church. What advice might you give to your friend about evaluating a church's worship service? Record your advice below, and base it on what you've learned about corporate worship services in this lesson.

NOTES

1. C. S. Lewis and Ayn Rand, as quoted by John Piper, *Desiring God*, 99, 101, available for viewing or download online at the Desiring God Web site.

2. This excerpt is from John Piper, *Gravity and Gladness* seminar notes, available online at the Desiring God Web site.

3. John Piper, "All of Life as Worship," an online sermon at the Desiring God Web site.

4. John Piper, *Brothers, We Are Not Professionals: A Plea to Pastors for Radical Ministry* (Nashville: Broadman & Holman, 2002), 39–40.

LESSON 9
ESSENTIAL ELEMENTS IN A WORSHIP SERVICE
A Companion Study to Gravity and Gladness, *Session 8*

LESSON OBJECTIVES

It is our prayer that after you have finished this lesson . . .

> You will be able to defend the idea that worship services are normative for local churches.

> You will begin to reflect on what the purpose of worship services is and what elements should comprise worship services.

> You will comprehend the place of preaching within worship services.

BEFORE YOU WATCH THE DVD, STUDY AND PREPARE

DAY 1: WORSHIP SERVICES AS NORMATIVE

Up until this point, we've mostly taken it for granted that Christians should be gathering together for corporate worship on a regular basis. In this lesson we will defend that assumption and then reflect on what elements should comprise a worship service.

QUESTION 1: Turn back to Question 1 of Lesson 3 and review the biblical passages listed there. Does the New Testament describe a pattern of corporate worship? If so, then how might that fact support the practice of corporate gatherings today?

*QUESTION 2: What would be lost if Christians stopped gathering together for worship?

We should worship together, not just privately.

Privately, YES! But not just privately. Psalm 149:1 says, "Sing to the LORD a new song, his praise in the assembly of the godly!" We are commanded to sing God's praises in the assembly of the godly—in the church!

Some may say, "I can worship God better by myself in the woods or by the lake." Perhaps you can. And God forbid that any of us should be denied our private encounters with God! But the test whether any experience of God is genuine or is simply an aesthetic high is whether it inclines you to obey God. If you don't come away from your private lakeside encounter more eager to meet God in the assembly of the faithful, you probably are not meeting God by the lake. If it were God, he would be filling your heart to obey his command to join with his people.

It IS a command of love, you know. If the deepest and highest joys could be had in private, the songs of heaven would be described as a solo here and a solo there instead of million-member choirs. So we should worship God together, not just in private.[1]

DAY 2: THE PURPOSE OF A WORSHIP SERVICE

To restate the central thesis of this seminar one more time, we've argued that the essential, vital, indispensable, defining heart of worship is the experience of being satisfied in God. We've also argued that godly affections for God are stirred up by a biblical vision of God.

*QUESTION 3: If it is true that the heart of worship is the experience of being satisfied in God and that affections for God are stirred up by truth about God, then what is the purpose of a worship service? What is the goal of a worship service, and what should be the means to accomplish that goal?

Here is an important assertion from John Piper about the forms of worship—that is, the songs, prayers, responsive readings, offerings, confessions, sermons, etc.

114

Forms of worship should provide two things: channels for the mind to apprehend the truth of God's reality and channels for the heart to respond to the beauty of that truth— that is, forms to ignite the affections with biblical truth and forms to express the affections with biblical passion.[2]

QUESTION 4: How do "channels for the mind" and "channels for the heart" (as described above) relate to the purpose of a worship service?

DAY 3: ELEMENTS IN A WORSHIP SERVICE

In the quote above, John Piper talks about "forms of worship" providing channels for the mind and heart. What forms, or elements, in a worship service will do this?

*QUESTION 5: Think about the worship service that you participated in (or led) this past Sunday. What forms or elements were a part of this worship service? List every element below, providing a brief description of each.

QUESTION 6: As you review the list you've just created, do each of these elements provide channels for the mind and heart to engage with God? Record your reflections below.

> So music and singing are necessary to Christian faith and worship for the simple reason that the realities of God and Christ, creation and salvation, heaven and hell are so great that when they are known truly and felt duly, they demand more than discussion and analysis and description; they demand poetry and song and music. Singing is the Christian's way of saying: God is so great that thinking will not suffice, there must be deep feeling; and talking will not suffice, there must be singing.[3]

DAY 4: PREACHING AS NORMATIVE

One of the typical elements in any evangelical worship service is the sermon. But is preaching the Word of God a *necessary* element of corporate worship? Could a mere reading of Scripture, a discussion about Scripture, or an artistic portrayal of Scripture substitute for the exposition and proclamation of Scripture? Are sermons appropriate for certain times and places and people, but not for others? In other words, is preaching *normative* for corporate worship in the local church?

Study Nehemiah 8:1–3, 6–9.

NEHEMIAH 8:1–3, 6–9

¹ And all the people gathered as one man into the square before the Water Gate. And they told Ezra the scribe to bring the Book of the Law of Moses that the LORD had commanded Israel. ² So Ezra the priest brought the Law before the assembly, both men and women and all who could understand what they heard, on the first day of the seventh month. ³ And he read from it facing the square before the Water Gate from early morning until midday, in the presence of the men and the women and those who could understand. And the ears of all the people were attentive to the Book of the Law. . . . ⁶ And Ezra blessed the LORD, the great God, and all the people answered, "Amen, Amen," lifting up their hands. And they bowed their heads and worshiped the LORD with their faces to the ground. ⁷ Also Jeshua, Bani, Sherebiah, Jamin, Akkub, Shabbethai, Hodiah, Maaseiah, Kelita, Azariah, Jozabad, Hanan, Pelaiah, the Levites, helped the people to understand the Law, while the people remained in their places. ⁸ They read from the book, from the Law of God, clearly, and they gave the sense, so that the people understood the reading. ⁹ And Nehemiah, who was the governor, and Ezra the priest and scribe, and the Levites who taught the people said to all the people, "This day is holy to the LORD your God; do not mourn or weep." For all the people wept as they heard the words of the Law.

QUESTION 7: What does this episode suggest about the practice of the old covenant community after the exile? How might this passage relate to modern-day corporate worship services?

Now study a passage in the New Testament about preaching the Word of God, 2 Timothy 3:16–4:4.

2 TIMOTHY 3:16–4:4

16 All Scripture is breathed out by God and profitable for teaching, for reproof, for correction, and for training in righteousness, 17 that the man of God may be competent, equipped for every good work.

4:1 I charge you in the presence of God and of Christ Jesus, who is to judge the living and the dead, and by his appearing and his kingdom: 2 preach the word; be ready in season and out of season; reprove, rebuke, and exhort, with complete patience and teaching. 3 For the time is coming when people will not endure sound teaching, but having itching ears they will accumulate for themselves teachers to suit their own passions, 4 and will turn away from listening to the truth and wander off into myths.

*QUESTION 8: According to this passage, how is preaching described? Why is it necessary?

In conclusion, then, the reason that preaching is so prominent in worship is that worship is not just understanding but also feeling. It is not just seeing God, but also savoring God. It is not just the response of the mind, but also of the heart. Therefore God has ordained that the form his Word should take in corporate worship is not just explanation to the mind and not just stimulation to the heart. Rather the Word of God is to come teaching the mind and reaching the heart; showing the truth of Christ and savoring the glory of Christ; exposing the Word of God and exulting in the God of the Word.

That is what preaching is. And that is why it is so prominent in worship. It is not a mere work of man. It is a gift and work of the Holy Spirit. And therefore it happens most and best where a people are praying and spiritually prepared for it.[4]

DAY 5: PREACHING AS WORSHIP

If preaching is to be a normative part of corporate worship, how is preaching related to worship? In other words, should preaching be considered part of the worship in a worship service?

QUESTION 9: How would you answer the question above? Is preaching worship? Why?

Read the following excerpts in which John Piper discusses the nature of worship and the nature of preaching. As you read, keep in mind the question of whether preaching should be considered worship.

There are always two parts to true worship. There is *seeing* God and there is *savoring* God. You can't separate these. You must see him to savor him. And if you don't savor him when you see him, you insult him. In true worship, there is always *understanding* with the mind and there is always *feeling* in the heart. . . .

The reason the Word of God takes the form of preaching in worship is that true preaching is the kind of speech that consistently unites these two aspects of worship, both in the way it is done and in the aims that it has. . . .

Preaching is a public exultation over the truth that it brings. It is not disinterested or cool or neutral. It is not mere explanation. It is manifestly and contagiously passionate about what it says. . . .

[Preaching] deals with the Word of God. True preaching is not the opinions of a mere man. It is the faithful exposition of God's Word. So in a phrase, preaching is *expository exultation*.

In conclusion, then, the reason that preaching is so essential to the corporate worship of the church is that it is uniquely suited to waken *seeing* God and *savoring* God. God has ordained that the Word of God come in a form that teaches the mind and reaches the heart.[5]

*QUESTION 10: According to these excerpts, how should the preacher worship as he preaches? And how should the congregation worship as they listen to the preaching?

FURTHER UP AND FURTHER IN

QUESTION 11: Copy below the list of elements in a worship service that you generated in response to Question 5 of this lesson. Then add to this list any other elements that you've observed in other worship services or potential elements to a worship service that you might imagine.

QUESTION 12: Now order this list from the previous question into three to six basic categories, according to what each element or activity is designed to accomplish. Is it important to incorporate elements from each basic category in every worship service?

Consider Ephesians 5:17–21.

EPHESIANS 5:17–21

> [17] Therefore do not be foolish, but understand what the will of the Lord is. [18] And do not get drunk with wine, for that is debauchery, but be filled with the Spirit, [19] addressing one

another in psalms and hymns and spiritual songs, singing and making melody to the Lord with your heart, [20] giving thanks always and for everything to God the Father in the name of our Lord Jesus Christ, [21] submitting to one another out of reverence for Christ.

QUESTION 13: Record five observations about this passage that could apply in some way to corporate worship.

    1.

    2.

    3.

    4.

    5.

Read or listen to John Piper, "Singing and Making Melody to the Lord," an online sermon at the Desiring God Web site.

QUESTION 14: List the six brief statements Piper makes about singing in corporate worship.

    1.

    2.

    3.

    4.

    5.

    6.

QUESTION 15: Compare your observations on Ephesians 5:17–21 (your answer to Question 13) to the six statements Piper makes about this passage (your answer to Question 14). What are three things that you have learned from reading or listening to Piper's sermon?

    1.

    2.

    3.

Lesson 9

WHILE YOU WATCH THE DVD, TAKE NOTES

Thesis #1: Regular corporate seasons (or services) of worship—the corporate act of honoring God by the pursuit of satisfaction in God through confession, supplication, thanks, and praise—are _____ for local churches.

Arguments for this claim:

Thesis #2: In these corporate services, confession, supplication, thanks, and praise will honor God in proportion to the intensity and authenticity of the _____ responding to the truth of God and his ways.

Thesis #3: In the real world of ordinary Christians, the pursuit of satisfaction of God does not usually arise in the hearts of God's people without being _____ _____ in some way when they come together.

Thesis #4: Therefore, essential to a corporate season is a fresh declaration of _____ about God and a fresh demonstration of affection for God.

Thesis #5: This fresh declaration of truth about God and a fresh demonstration of affection for God honor God most and help people honor him best when they happen not only in song but also in _____. In other words, we should not conceive of the service as separated into instruction (teaching and lecture) and inspiration (music and testimony). The _____ should be expository exultation and thus an act of worship.

Thesis #6: There is biblical evidence from the time of Ezra to Jesus to the synagogue to the beginnings of the Christian church that corporate worship included _____.

Thesis #7: Therefore, preaching as worship, or preaching as expository exultation, is a normative element in worship services.

123

AFTER YOU WATCH THE DVD, DISCUSS WHAT YOU'VE LEARNED

1) Which argument did you find most convincing for why corporate seasons of worship are normative for local churches?

2) Why is it harmful to say, "We worship for thirty minutes and then there's preaching"? Why does Piper feel so strongly that a worship service should be "seamless"? What does he mean by this word?

3) Which thesis out of the seven was the most provocative for you? Which thesis was the most confusing?

AFTER YOU DISCUSS, MAKE APPLICATION

1) What was the most meaningful part of this lesson for you? Was there a sentence, concept, or idea that really struck you? Why? Record your thoughts in the space below.

2) Suppose you were a member at a church that was looking for a "worship pastor" or "worship leader." If you were asked to be on the search committee for that position, for what characteristics in a worship pastor would you advocate? What things would be important to you, and what things might be less important? Explain your answers.

NOTES

1. John Piper, "You Shall Worship the Lord Your God," an online sermon at the Desiring God Web site.
2. John Piper, *Desiring God*, 104, available for viewing or download online at the Desiring God Web site.
3. John Piper, "Singing and Making Melody to the Lord," an online sermon at the Desiring God Web site.
4. John Piper, "The Place of Preaching in Worship," an online sermon at the Desiring God Web site.
5. John Piper, *The Supremacy of God in Preaching* (rev. ed.; Grand Rapids: Baker Books, 2004), 10–11.

LESSON 10

A PHILOSOPHY OF MUSIC AND WORSHIP, PART 1

A Companion Study to Gravity and Gladness, *Session 9*

LESSON OBJECTIVES

It is our prayer that after you have finished this lesson . . .

> You will begin to think about what should unite your church in worship.

> You will engage with Bethlehem Baptist Church's philosophy of music and worship.

> You will reflect on Piper's call for gravity and gladness on Sunday mornings.

BEFORE YOU WATCH THE DVD, STUDY AND PREPARE

DAY 1: UNITY ON A DEEP LEVEL

A thousand decisions need to be made about corporate worship on Sunday mornings. Praise songs or hymns? Drums or an organ? Pews or chairs? Dress up or dress down? Standing or sitting or kneeling or lifting hands? Projector? Wooden pulpit? Carpet color? When to do announcements? What to do with children? How long is the sermon? How loud are the amplifiers? What translation of the Bible? *How is it possible for everyone to agree on all these decisions?*

QUESTION 1: Is it possible for everyone in a church to agree on all matters of form and style? If not, how is unity to be achieved?

Examine the following biblical passages concerning unity.

PSALM 133

¹ Behold, how good and pleasant it is when brothers dwell in unity! ² It is like the precious oil on the head, running down on the beard, on the beard of Aaron, running down on the collar of his robes! ³ It is like the dew of Hermon, which falls on the mountains of Zion! For there the LORD has commanded the blessing, life forevermore.

EPHESIANS 4:1–6

¹ I therefore, a prisoner for the Lord, urge you to walk in a manner worthy of the calling to which you have been called, ² with all humility and gentleness, with patience, bearing with one another in love, ³ eager to maintain the unity of the Spirit in the bond of peace. ⁴ There is one body and one Spirit—just as you were called to the one hope that belongs to your call— ⁵ one Lord, one faith, one baptism, ⁶ one God and Father of all, who is over all and through all and in all.

PHILIPPIANS 2:1–4

[1] So if there is any encouragement in Christ, any comfort from love, any participation in the Spirit, any affection and sympathy, [2] complete my joy by being of the same mind, having the same love, being in full accord and of one mind. [3] Do nothing from rivalry or conceit, but in humility count others more significant than yourselves. [4] Let each of you look not only to his own interests, but also to the interests of others.

1 PETER 3:8

Finally, all of you, have unity of mind, sympathy, brotherly love, a tender heart, and a humble mind.

*QUESTION 2: What observations can you make about biblical unity from these passages? How might this apply to the so-called "worship wars"?

DAY 2: GOING VERTICAL

Every worship service will have elements that are more "vertically" oriented and those that are more "horizontally" oriented. "Vertical" elements are activities in which the participants in the worship service are focused primarily on God himself and in which the human-to-human relationships within the congregation are not emphasized. "Horizontal" elements are those activities in which people focus on the other human participants who are a part of the worship service.

QUESTION 3: Given these descriptions of "vertical" and "horizontal" elements within a worship service, list as many examples of each as you can think of.

Vertical Elements   **Horizontal Elements**

*QUESTION 4: In your opinion, should a worship service have primarily a vertical focus or a horizontal focus, or should there be an equal balance between the two? Explain your reasons.

DAY 3: OOZING SCRIPTURE ON SUNDAYS

In Question 5 of the previous lesson (Lesson 9), we asked you to think about the worship service that you participated in most recently. The design of this question was not to foster a harsh, critical, or arrogant spirit, but rather to promote healthy reflection. This next question requires a similar exercise, and once again we hope that you approach it in a constructive and humble spirit.

*QUESTION 5: Think about the worship service that you participated in (or led) this past Sunday. What elements were a part of this worship service? List every element below, and note what role (if any) Scripture had in each element. Was Scripture quoted explicitly and deliberately?

In the video session corresponding to this lesson, John Piper will draw the distinction between being "Bible based" and "Bible saturated" in a worship service.

QUESTION 6: Before hearing Piper's discussion of this distinction, what distinction do you think he might make between these two terms? In other words, what difference might you anticipate between being "Bible based" and "Bible saturated" in a corporate worship service?

DAY 4: BEING BLOOD-EARNEST

It is no secret that one of John Piper's heroes in the faith is Jonathan Edwards. Here is a description that Sereno Dwight gave of Edwards:

> One of the positive causes of his . . . great success as a preacher, was the deep and pervading solemnity of his mind. He had, at all times, a solemn consciousness of the presence of God. This was visible in his looks and his demeanor. It obviously had a controlling influence over all his preparations for the pulpit; and was most manifest in all his public services. Its effect on the audience was immediate and not to be resisted.[1]

John Piper then makes these comments about Jonathan Edwards:

> Intensity of feeling, the weight of argument, a deep and pervading solemnity of mind, a savor of the power of godliness, fervency of spirit, zeal for God—these are the marks of the "gravity of preaching." If there is one thing we can learn from Jonathan Edwards, it is to take our calling seriously, not to trifle with the Word of God and the act of preaching.[2]

*QUESTION 7: Do you believe that a "deep and pervading solemnity" should characterize the preaching in corporate worship? Should it characterize the rest of the service as well? Explain the reasons for your answers.

Piper once again gives his diagnosis of worship services and preaching in our day.

If you endeavor to bring a holy hush upon your people in a worship service, you can be assured that someone will say that the atmosphere is unfriendly or cold. All that many people can imagine is that the absence of chatter would mean the presence of stiffness and awkwardness and unfriendliness. Since they have little or no experience of the deep gladness of momentous moments of gravity, they strive for gladness the only way they know how — by being lighthearted and chipper and talkative.

Pastors have absorbed this narrow view of gladness and friendliness and now cultivate it across the land with pulpit demeanor and verbal casualness that make the blood-earnestness of Chalmers and the pervading solemnity of Edwards's mind unthinkable. The result is a preaching atmosphere and a preaching style plagued by triviality, levity, carelessness, flippancy, and a general spirit that nothing of eternal and infinite proportions is being done or said on Sunday morning.

If I were to put my thesis into a measured sentence it would go like this: *Gladness and gravity should be woven together in the life and preaching of a pastor in such a way as to sober the careless soul and sweeten the burdens of the saints.*[3]

QUESTION 8: Write your own description of what gravity and gladness would look like if woven together in corporate worship services.

DAY 5: SLAPSTICK ON SUNDAY MORNINGS

An issue that is related to blood-earnestness in worship services is the place of humor on Sunday mornings. Is it appropriate to tell jokes on Sunday mornings?

> God saves people from everlasting ruin through preaching. . . . This is simply stupendous to think about—that when I preach, the everlasting destiny of sinners hangs in the balance! If a person is not made earnest and grave by this fact, people will unconsciously learn that the realities of heaven and hell are not serious. And I can't help but think that this is what is being communicated by the casual cleverness that comes from so many pulpits. James Denney said, "No man can give the impression that he himself is clever and that Christ is mighty to save." John Henry Jowett said, "We never reach the innermost room in any man's soul by the expediencies of the showman or the buffoon." And yet today it seems to be the stock in trade of many preachers that they must say something cute or clever or funny.[4]

QUESTION 9: Once again, does what Piper writes about preaching apply more broadly to worship services in general? If so, how?

*QUESTION 10: List five adjectives that describe the tone of what you think worship services should be. Then list five adjectives that you think should *not* describe the tone of what worship services should be.

> I was at a gathering recently where we were worshiping. The pianist was very accomplished. It was obvious. But he had led us into the presence of the Lord and most of us really were singing to the Lord and dealing with God. Another act of worship was to follow this song that would have kept us in conscious communion with God. But as the hymn came to an end, the person who was to lead us into the next act of worship looked at the pianist and said, "There is living proof that all men are not created equal." A few people chuckled. And then he tried to reintroduce communion with God.
>
> That sort of thing is what I grew up on. And many of you did. And it's why we never learned what it is to go hard after God in worship. It's why a sustained communion with God in corporate worship is a foreign experience for most people. And yet when most Christians taste it, they sense that they have come into something that they have missed and that is needed in the core of their lives.[5]

FURTHER UP AND FURTHER IN
Read or listen to John Piper, "Ambushing Satan with Song," an online sermon at the Desiring God Web site.

QUESTION 11: Record in one sentence what you take to be the main thesis of this sermon. How does John Piper support this thesis with Scripture and testimony?

QUESTION 12: What precedent does John Piper see for a church choir? According to Piper, what is the choir supposed to do?

Read John Piper, "A Case for Seriousness," an online article at the Desiring God Web site.

QUESTION 13: How would you answer the question that concludes this article?

Read or listen to John Piper, "Amen," an online sermon at the Desiring God Web site.

QUESTION 14: Summarize what John Piper says about this little word. What does this word mean according to the Bible, and how was it used?

QUESTION 15: Do you say "Amen" during corporate prayer, singing, or preaching? Should you? Why or why not?

Here is an exhortation that John Piper has given to Bethlehem Baptist Church regarding this issue:

> The spirit of worship at Bethlehem is so different than what many people are used to that they don't know quite what to make of it. Often wrong conclusions are jumped to. For example, one may think: Well, since they don't announce the hymns, and they discourage conversation during the prelude, and everything on the platform seems to be thought through ahead of time, they probably don't want any spontaneous involvement at all.
>
> But that is a wrong conclusion. The goal is to meet God together. Every part of the service is designed either to channel God's reality to you or to channel your affections to God. There are, of course, a lot of spontaneous things

that you could do that would derail this locomotive of worship. But there are also some that would not derail us but would in fact stoke the engine.

For example, there is nothing in our concept of worship to hinder a hearty "Amen!" when your heart beats with what is said or sung. Why must I go down to preach at Bethesda Baptist in order to hear a chorus of Amens? I can tell by your faces often when it's on the tip of your tongue. Let it out! Be expressive. Who knows what might get pulled out of this preacher or this choir! Visitors need to know whether anyone here really agrees with and loves what this preacher is saying and the choir is singing. Your nods and ummhmms and Amens and your posture of attention bear witness that this is a shared message, not just a one-man stand.[6]

And here is another:

I think some of you have gotten wrong signals from me and Bruce. Two people recently asked me what I would feel like if they said "Amen!" when something moved them. Now the only reason anyone would ask that is if they are getting wrong signals. The answer is: We would feel great! It's the same with lifting your hands in praise. When it is in your heart, *do it!* Anything that helps you express your heart for God and does not hinder other people is OK with us. We want *life* in the sanctuary on Sunday.

Listen, I really mean this. There is not much that would delight me more than a hundred people so in tune with my preaching that when my heart said, "This is great," your voice said "Amen!" Not only would it tell me that our hearts are in tune, it would witness to visitors and lifeless members that there is more than one person here excited about this great Gospel. An electric atmosphere of worship could happen during the sermon if you joined me in it—even if only with a moved moan or an agreeable "ummhmm."[7]

WHILE YOU WATCH THE DVD, TAKE NOTES
A period of history in Bethlehem's corporate worship

"Unity and solutions to practical problems often come from deep _____ [on a philosophy of music and worship]."

What unites Bethlehem in worship
1.

"We have 168 hours in a week . . . is it excessive that one of those hours would be radically _____?"

2.

3.

4. Bible based and Bible _____.

5.

6.

AFTER YOU WATCH THE DVD, DISCUSS WHAT YOU'VE LEARNED

1) Did anything in Piper's description of Bethlehem's history resonate with your own experience of corporate worship in churches in which you've been involved?

2) Are the six points of music and worship philosophy presented in this session connected to what Piper has taught in previous sessions? If so, how?

3) Do you agree with the points that Piper presents? Why or why not? Does your church's worship service reflect the same priorities that Bethlehem holds?

AFTER YOU DISCUSS, MAKE APPLICATION

1) What was the most meaningful part of this lesson for you? Was there a sentence, concept, or idea that really struck you? Why? Record your thoughts in the space below.

2) Piper has presented six out of the eleven things that he wants to unite Bethlehem Baptist Church in worship. In the next session Piper will present the five remaining

points. If you were teaching this seminar, with what five points would you conclude? In other words, what points regarding a philosophy of music and worship do you think still need to be mentioned after the six that already have been? Record five points below and your reasons for including these things.

1.

2.

3.

4.

5.

NOTES

1. Sereno Dwight, as quoted by John Piper in *Desiring God*, 53, available for viewing or download online at the Desiring God Web site.

2. Ibid., 54.

3. Ibid.

4. Ibid., 58–59.

5. John Piper, "Prepare to Meet Your God," an online sermon at the Desiring God Web site.

6. John Piper, "You Shall Worship the Lord Your God," an online sermon at the Desiring God Web site.

7. John Piper, "Is It OK to Say *Amen!* on Sunday?" an online article at the Desiring God Web site.

LESSON 11
A PHILOSOPHY OF MUSIC AND WORSHIP, PART 2
A Companion Study to Gravity and Gladness, *Session 10*

LESSON OBJECTIVES

It is our prayer that after you have finished this lesson . . .

> You will continue to think about what should unite your church in worship.

> You will apply the principle of "undistracting excellence" to your own corporate worship service.

> You will consider Piper's practical preparations for Sunday mornings.

BEFORE YOU WATCH THE DVD, STUDY AND PREPARE

DAY 1: AUTHENTICITY IN WORSHIP SERVICES

This lesson will continue the presentation of Bethlehem Baptist Church's philosophy of music and worship. Our aim in doing this is to spur your own thinking about what is biblical, appropriate, wise, and helpful to do in the corporate worship services in which you participate.

Study 1 Peter 1:22, Romans 12:9, and 2 Corinthians 4:2.

1 PETER 1:22

Having purified your souls by your obedience to the truth for a sincere brotherly love, love one another earnestly from a pure heart.

ROMANS 12:9

Let love be genuine. Abhor what is evil; hold fast to what is good.

2 CORINTHIANS 4:2

But we have renounced disgraceful, underhanded ways. We refuse to practice cunning or to tamper with God's word, but by the open statement of the truth we would commend ourselves to everyone's conscience in the sight of God.

QUESTION 1: How might these verses be applied in corporate worship services? Be specific in your answer.

Here are some of Piper's desires for his own church:

My heart's desire for Bethlehem is that we might become a people known for our sense of ultimate reality. I want people to visit Bethlehem and say, "Those people seem to take their worship so seriously. They seem to be so aware of God. They seem to be living on the brink of something infinite. Nobody seems to be playing church or going through motions. You get the impression this could be their last time together before they die. You have the feeling something awesome is at stake."

O that our worship might come alive with the incredible presence of the living Christ! Pray that God might free us all from worship games. Come to meet the living God! These are precious days together at Bethlehem. None of us knows when it will be our last Sunday in the house of the Lord. Drink deep in worship. Picture yourself on the brink of eternity. Space falls away infinitely before you. And you say, "I see Jesus! I see Jesus! The choir of heaven! The choir of heaven!"[1]

*QUESTION 2: What are some examples of what Piper calls "playing church" or "worship games"? How do these things rob a worship service of its authenticity?

DAY 2: "UNDISTRACTING EXCELLENCE"

We've encountered the phrase "undistracting excellence" already in Lesson 8. Here are some comments of appreciation that John Piper wrote for two pastors' wives who also are pianists:

> Whether it is worship services, weddings, funerals, or other gatherings, Carol and Vicki are models of undistracting excellence. That is, they do their work so well they are almost invisible. There is no distracting flare. There is rock-solid strength in the genre at hand, and I never lose a moment's peace worrying about their competence or their appropriateness.[2]

*QUESTION 3: Why might John Piper be so thankful that these pianists are "almost invisible"?

Now examine 1 Corinthians 2:2–5.

1 CORINTHIANS 2:2-5

> [2] For I decided to know nothing among you except Jesus Christ and him crucified. [3] And I was with you in weakness and in fear and much trembling, [4] and my speech and my message were not in plausible words of wisdom, but in demonstration of the Spirit and of power, [5] that your faith might not rest in the wisdom of men but in the power of God.

QUESTION 4: Describe what "undistracting excellence" looks like in preaching.

What Paul wanted more than anything in his life was to get out of the way of the power of God. The thought that anyone might pin their hope or their faith on his eloquence or his strength was a dreadful thought to Paul. All he wanted was to placard Christ crucified so that the power of the cross could save sinners.

And so what did he do? He died on the cross every day. He died to intellectual show. He died to impressive eloquence. He died to the secular demands of suave, self-assured, powerful, attractive performances.

He was with us in weakness and in much fear and trembling so that our faith—yours and mine, this morning—might rest not in the wisdom of a man, but in the power of God—the power of Christ crucified.[3]

DAY 3: WELCOMING OTHERS IN WORSHIP

Should a church intentionally pursue ethnic diversity in its corporate worship service? Here is a statement of Bethlehem's policy:

> Over ten years ago, we at Bethlehem set ourselves on a trajectory of intentional ethnic diversity. It coheres with the emphasis on "the joy of all peoples" in our mission statement: *We exist to spread a passion for the supremacy of God in all things* **for the**

joy of all peoples through Jesus Christ. But we did not make it easy for ourselves. It would be easy if we said, "Diversity is the top priority that outweighs all others." Or: "Diversity at any cost." But there are things more important than ethnic diversity.

*QUESTION 5: How might God be glorified by ethnic diversity in corporate worship?

QUESTION 6: If a church was committed to pursuing ethnic diversity, what things might change about its worship services? What things shouldn't change?

DAY 4: TAKE HEED HOW YOU HEAR

Throughout this seminar, John Piper has reinforced the seriousness, gravity, and solemnity that should characterize a Christian worship service. This applies not only to those leading worship (whether singers, readers, or preachers), but also to those in the congregation who are singing and listening.

Read Luke 8:4–15, 18.

LUKE 8:4–15, 18

⁴ And when a great crowd was gathering and people from town after town came to him, he said in a parable: ⁵ "A sower went out to sow his seed. And as he sowed, some fell along the path and was trampled underfoot, and the birds of the air devoured it. ⁶ And some fell on the rock, and as it grew up, it withered away, because it had no moisture. ⁷ And some fell among thorns, and the thorns grew up with it and choked it. ⁸ And some fell into good soil and grew and yielded a hundredfold." As he said these things, he called out, "He who has ears to hear, let him hear." ⁹ And when his disciples asked him what this parable meant, ¹⁰ he said, "To you it has been given to know the secrets of the kingdom of God, but for others they are in parables, so that 'seeing they may not see, and hearing they may not understand.' ¹¹ Now the parable is this: The seed is the word of God. ¹² The ones along the path are those who have heard; then the devil comes and takes away the word from their hearts, so that they may not believe and be saved. ¹³ And the ones on the rock are those who, when they hear the word, receive it with joy. But these have no root; they believe for a while, and in time of testing fall away. ¹⁴ And as for what fell among the thorns, they are those who hear, but as they go on their way they are choked by the cares and riches and pleasures of life, and their fruit does not mature. ¹⁵ As for that in the good soil, they are those who, hearing the word, hold it fast in an honest and good heart, and bear fruit with patience. . . . ¹⁸ Take care then how you hear, for to the one who has, more will be given, and from the one who has not, even what he thinks that he has will be taken away."

QUESTION 7: How does Jesus' exhortation to "take care then how you hear" relate to the parable he tells and his explanation of it?

*QUESTION 8: How might Jesus' teaching in this passage apply to corporate worship?

> Hearing is huge. I believe with all my heart that I am called to preach the Word of God. And many of you are called to teach it in various settings. But this text is about another great calling—the calling to hear the Word of God. And it is no small thing. The stakes are very high. There is a hearing that barely gets started and the Word is gone before you get out the door. There is a hearing that lasts until there is a hard time in life, and then one turns from God to other messages. There is a hearing that flourishes until the riches and pleasures of this life choke it off. And there is a hearing that defeats the devil, endures trial, scorns riches and bears fruit unto eternal life.[4]

DAY 5: AGAIN, TAKE HEED HOW YOU HEAR!

In the DVD session that accompanies this lesson, Piper will share ten practical preparations for hearing the Word of God on Sunday morning. We want to list these ten preparations here now, before you hear Piper speak about them:

1. Pray that God would give you a good and honest heart.

2. Meditate on the Word of God.

3. Purify your mind by turning away from worldly entertainment.

4. Trust in the truth that you already have.

5. Rest long enough Saturday night to be alert and hopeful Sunday morning.

6. Forebear one another Sunday morning without grumbling and criticism.

7. Be meek and teachable when you come.

8. Be still as you enter the room, and focus your mind's attention and heart's affection on God.

9. Think earnestly about what is sung and prayed and preached.

10. Desire the truth of God's Word more than you desire riches or food.

*QUESTION 9: As you read over this list, do any of Piper's suggestions confuse you? Which practical preparation would you most like to put into practice?

QUESTION 10: Can you think of any practical preparations for Sunday morning that Piper doesn't mention in his list of ten? Think of as many as you can and write them below.

The ascended Lord Jesus Christ said to the church at Laodicea, "Would that you were either cold or hot! So, because you are lukewarm, and neither hot nor cold, I will spit you out of my mouth" (Revelation 3:15–16). Is it not consistent with the image to say that lukewarm worship turns the stomach of Christ?

This is why Saturday night and early Sunday morning preparation is so important before you come to worship. It's why the prelude is indispensable. We are not naturally hot. We must trim the wick with the Word of God. We must seek the breath of his Spirit to blow it into a flame. He will not quench a smoldering flax! If we seek him!

Brothers and sisters, we must be more earnest in seeking God in worship. We must be less flippant and less frivolous and thoughtless and casual and disrespectful as we approach the chamber of God in the assembly of the faithful.[5]

FURTHER UP AND FURTHER IN

John Piper narrates his experience on one Saturday night before church the next morning:

Last Saturday night at about 10:30 I came up from working on my sermon in the basement and asked Noël if she wanted to take a walk around the block. The air was cool and the moving clouds were letting the stars in and out. We locked the door behind us and started down the front steps. I looked over to my next-door neighbor's house and through his wide-open window saw a big color TV screen. And on it I saw a girl dancing. Her movements and her clothes were clearly intended to be sexually arousing.

Noël and I began our walk in silence. Then I turned to her and said, "I wonder how many of our people at Bethlehem are preparing themselves for worship tomorrow by watching that show?" As we walked in the quietness I thought back to my teenage years when I used to gorge myself on television. I thought about all those Saturday nights when I religiously positioned myself in the pew of our domestic sanctuary with a box of Wheaties to watch *Hootenanny*, *Have Gun Will Travel*, *Gunsmoke* and the news and weather. I remember later at college looking back somewhat rudely and complaining that our church had not provided any really meaningful Sunday morning worship times. Now I look back with repentance and tears. It seems so obvious to me now. All rich and meaningful experiences require preparation and expectancy.[6]

QUESTION 11: Meditate on Piper's concluding assertion: "All rich and meaningful experiences require preparation and expectancy." Do you agree with this? Explain. What implications does this statement have for corporate worship services?

Read John Piper, "Thoughts on Worship and Culture," an online article at the Desiring God Web site.

In this *Gravity and Gladness* seminar, Piper chose not to invest time in discussing the differences between what he calls "fine culture" and "folk culture." This distinction, however, can be very helpful in planning and evaluating corporate worship services. Therefore, the final four questions of this lesson will be devoted to provoking thought on worship and culture.

QUESTION 12: According to Piper's article, what is fine culture? How would you describe it, and what are its intrinsic vulnerabilities and potential positives? Record your notes below.

QUESTION 13: What is folk culture? How would you describe it, and what are its intrinsic vulnerabilities and potential positives? Record your notes below.

QUESTION 14: In this article, Piper claims that "in the church all that we do falls somewhere on the continuum between fine culture and folk culture." Think about your own church, and list examples below of expressions of fine culture and expressions of folk culture.

Expressions of Fine Culture   Expressions of Folk Culture

QUESTION 15: According to the table above, does your church achieve a good balance between fine and folk culture? If so, what might your church do to strengthen its mixed "culture"? If not, how might your church express its worship in both "high" and "low" cultural ways?

WHILE YOU WATCH THE DVD, TAKE NOTES

What unites Bethlehem in worship

7.

8.

9.

"We'll try to sing and play and pray and preach in such a way that people's attention will not be diverted from the substance by _____ ministry or by excessive _____."

10.

11.

Ten practical preparations for hearing the Word of God on Sunday morning

"We've talked mostly about our hearts and about the inner nature of true, authentic worship here and that's because I think that's just the _____ the Bible has and the New Testament especially."

AFTER YOU WATCH THE DVD, DISCUSS WHAT YOU'VE LEARNED

1) Compare Piper's five points in this session to the five points you wrote down for application at the conclusion to Lesson 10. Are your points similar to his or different?

2) Have you found that Piper's teaching in this seminar has been relevant to some of the specific issues of form and style in corporate worship with which your church might be wrestling?

3) After hearing Piper share his ten practical preparations for Sunday morning, did you find any of his suggestions particularly challenging or convicting? Why?

AFTER YOU DISCUSS, MAKE APPLICATION

1) What was the most meaningful part of this lesson for you? Was there a sentence, concept, or idea that really struck you? Why? Record your thoughts in the space below.

2) In reviewing what you've learned through the seminar and this study guide, write down one thing that you would like to share with the leadership of your own church regarding corporate worship services on Sunday mornings (or at other times). Why do you want to share this particular comment or observation? Then share it with them in humility and love.

NOTES

1. John Piper, "On Princeton and Worship," an online article at the Desiring God Web site.
2. John Piper, "Thanking God for Ten Years of Partnership in the Gospel," an online sermon at the Desiring God Web site.
3. John Piper, "The Present Power of Christ Crucified," an online sermon at the Desiring God Web site.
4. John Piper, "Take Care How You Listen! Part 1," an online sermon at the Desiring God Web site.
5. John Piper, "You Shall Worship the Lord Your God," an online sermon at the Desiring God Web site.
6. John Piper, "Saturday Night at the Manse," an online article at the Desiring God Web site.

LESSON 12
REVIEW AND CONCLUSION

LESSON OBJECTIVES

It is our prayer that after you have finished this lesson . . .

> You will be able to summarize and synthesize what you've learned.

> You will hear what others in your group have learned.

> You will share with others how you have begun to put into practice the biblical vision of worship and corporate gatherings.

WHAT HAVE YOU LEARNED?

There are no study questions to answer in preparation for this lesson. Instead spend your time writing a few paragraphs that explain what you've learned in this group study. To help you do this, you may choose to review the notes you've taken in the previous lessons. Then, after you've written down what you've learned, write down some questions that still remain in your mind about anything addressed in these lessons. Be prepared to share these reflections and questions with the group in the next lesson.

NOTES

Use this space to record anything in the group discussion that you want to remember.

LEADER'S GUIDE

AS THE LEADER OF THIS GROUP STUDY, **it is imperative that you are completely familiar with this study guide** and with the *Gravity and Gladness* DVD Set. Therefore, it is our strong recommendation that you (1) read and understand the introduction, (2) skim each lesson, surveying its layout and content, and (3) read the entire Leader's Guide *before* you begin the group study and distribute the study guides. As you review this Leader's Guide, keep in mind that the material here is only a recommendation. As the leader of the study, feel free to adapt this study guide to your situation and context.

BEFORE LESSON 1

Before the first lesson, you will need to know approximately how many participants you will have in your group study. **Each participant will need his or her own study guide!** Therefore, be sure to order enough study guides. You will distribute these study guides at the beginning of the first lesson.

It is also our strong recommendation that you, as the leader, familiarize yourself with this study guide and the *Gravity and Gladness* DVD Set in order to answer any questions that might arise and also to ensure that each group session runs smoothly and maximizes the learning of the participants. It is not necessary for you to preview *Gravity and Gladness* in its entirety—although it certainly wouldn't hurt!—but you should be prepared to navigate your way through each DVD menu.

DURING LESSON 1

Each lesson is designed for a one-hour group session. Lessons 2–12 require preparatory work from the participant before this group session. Lesson 1, however, requires no preparation on the part of the participant.

The following schedule is how we suggest that you use the first hour of your group study:

INTRODUCTION TO THE STUDY GUIDE (10 MINUTES)

Introduce this study guide and the *Gravity and Gladness* DVD. Share with the group why you chose to lead the group study using these resources. Inform your group of the commitment that this study will require and motivate them to work hard. Pray for the twelve-week study, asking God for the grace you will need. Then distribute one study guide to each participant. You may read the introduction aloud, if you want, or you may immediately turn the group to Lesson 1 (starting on page 11 of this study guide).

PERSONAL INTRODUCTIONS (15 MINUTES)

Since group discussion will be an integral part of this guided study, it is crucial that each participant feels welcome and safe. The goal of each lesson is for every participant to contribute to the discussion in some way. Therefore, during this fifteen minutes, have each participant introduce himself or herself. You may choose to use the questions listed in the section entitled "About Yourself" or you may ask questions of your own choosing.

DISCUSSION (25 MINUTES)

Transition from the time of introductions to the discussion questions listed under the heading "A Preview of *Gravity and Gladness*." Invite everyone in the class to respond to these questions, but don't let the discussion become too involved. These questions are designed to spark interest and generate questions. The aim is not to come to definitive answers yet.

REVIEW AND CLOSING (10 MINUTES)

End the group session by reviewing Lesson 2 with the group participants and informing them of the preparation that they must do before the group meets again. Encourage them to be faithful in preparing for the next lesson. Answer any questions that the group may have and then close in prayer.

BEFORE LESSONS 2–11

As the group leader, you should do all the preparation for each lesson that is required of the group participants, that is, the ten study questions. Furthermore, it is highly recommended that you complete the entire "Further Up and Further In" section. This is not required of the group participants, but it will enrich your preparation and will help you guide and shape the conversation more effectively.

The group leader should also preview the session of *Gravity and Gladness* that will be covered in the next lesson. So, for example, if the group participants are doing the preparatory work for Lesson 3, you should preview *Gravity and Gladness*, Session 2 before the group meets and views it. Previewing each session will better equip you to understand the material and answer questions. If you want to pause the DVD in the midst of the session in order to clarify or discuss, previewing the session will allow you to plan where you want to take your pauses.

Finally, you may want to supplement or modify the discussion questions or the application assignment. Please remember that **this study guide is a resource**; any additions or changes you make that better match the study to your particular group are encouraged. As the group leader, your own discernment, creativity, and guidance are invaluable, and you should adapt the material as you see fit.

Plan for about two hours of your own preparation before each lesson!

DURING LESSONS 2–11

Again, let us stress that during Lessons 2–11 you may use the group time in whatever way you desire. The following schedule, however, is what we suggest:

DISCUSSION (15 MINUTES)

Begin your time with prayer. The tone you set in your prayer will likely be impressed upon the group participants: if your prayer is serious and heartfelt, the group participants will be serious about prayer; if your prayer is hasty, sloppy, or a token gesture, the group participants will share this same attitude toward prayer. So model the kind of praying that you desire your students to imitate. Remember, the blood of Jesus has bought your access to the throne of grace.

After praying, review the preparatory work that the participants completed. How did they answer the questions? Which questions did they find to be the most interesting or the most confusing?

What observations or insights can they share with the group? If you would like to review some tips for leading productive discussion, please turn to appendix B at the end of this study guide.

The group participants will be provided an opportunity to apply what they've learned in Lessons 2–11. As the group leader, you can choose whether it would be appropriate for the group to discuss these assignments during this fifteen-minute time slot.

DVD VIEWING (25 MINUTES)[1]

Play the session for *Gravity and Gladness* that corresponds to the lesson you're studying. You may choose to pause the DVD at crucial points to check for understanding and provide clarification. Or you may choose to watch the DVD without interruption.

DISCUSSION AND CLOSING (20 MINUTES)

Foster discussion on what was taught during John Piper's session. You may do this by first reviewing the DVD notes (under the heading "While You Watch the DVD, Take Notes") and then proceeding to the discussion questions, listed under the heading "After You Watch the DVD, Discuss What You've Learned." These discussion questions are meant to be springboards that launch the group into further and deeper discussion. Don't feel constrained to these questions if the group discussion begins to move in other helpful directions.

Close the time by briefly reviewing the application section and the homework that is expected for the next lesson. Pray and dismiss.

BEFORE LESSON 12

It is important that you encourage the group participants to complete the preparatory work for Lesson 12. This assignment invites the participants to reflect on what they've learned and what remaining questions they still have. As the group leader, this would be a helpful assignment for you to complete as well. In addition, you may want to write down the key concepts of this DVD series that you want the group participants to walk away with.

DURING LESSON 12

The group participants are expected to complete a reflection exercise as part of their preparation for Lesson 12. The bulk of the group time during this last lesson should be focused on reviewing and synthesizing what was learned. Encourage all participants to share some of their recorded thoughts. Attempt to answer any remaining questions that they might have.

To close this last lesson, you might want to spend extended time in prayer. If appropriate, take prayer requests relating to what the participants have learned in these ten weeks, and bring these requests to God.

It would be completely appropriate for you, the group leader, to give a final charge or word of exhortation to end this group study. Speak from your heart and out of the overflow of joy that you have in God.

Please receive our blessing for all you group leaders who choose to use this study guide:

> The LORD bless you and keep you; the LORD make his face to shine upon you and be gracious to you; the LORD lift up his countenance upon you and give you peace. (Numbers 6:24–26)

NOTES

1. Twenty-five minutes is only an approximation. Some of the sessions are shorter, while some are longer. You may need to budget your group time differently, depending upon which session you are viewing.

APPENDIX A
SIX-SESSION INTENSIVE OPTION

WE UNDERSTAND THAT THERE ARE circumstances that may prohibit a group from devoting twelve sessions to this study. In view of this, we have designed a six-session intensive option for groups that need to complete the material in less time. In the intensive option, the group should meet for two hours each week. Here is our suggestion for how to complete the material in six weeks:

Week 1 Introduction to the Study Guide and Lesson 1
Week 2 Lessons 2 and 3 (DVD Sessions 1 and 2)
Week 3 Lessons 4 and 5 (DVD Sessions 3 and 4)
Week 4 Lessons 6 and 7 (DVD Sessions 5 and 6)
Week 5 Lessons 8 and 9 (DVD Sessions 7 and 8)
Week 6 Lessons 10 and 11 (DVD Sessions 9 and 10)

Notice that we have not included Lesson 12 in the intensive option. Moreover, because each participant is required to complete two lessons per week, it will be necessary to combine the number of "days" within each lesson so that all of the material is covered. Thus, for example, during Week 2 in the intensive option, each participant will complete

> Lesson 2, Days 1 and 2, on the first day;
> Lesson 2, Days 3 and 4, on the second day;

❯ Lesson 2, Day 5, and Lesson 3, Day 1, on the third day;

❯ Lesson 3, Days 2 and 3, on the fourth day;

❯ Lesson 3, Days 4 and 5, on the fifth day.

Because of the amount of material, we recommend that students focus on questions marked with an asterisk (*) first, and then, if time permits, complete the rest of the questions.

APPENDIX B

LEADING PRODUCTIVE DISCUSSIONS

Note: This material has been adapted from curricula produced by The Bethlehem Institute (TBI), a ministry of Bethlehem Baptist Church. It is used by permission.

IT IS OUR CONVICTION THAT the best group leaders foster an environment in their group that engages the participants. Most people learn by solving problems or by working through things that provoke curiosity or concern. Therefore, we discourage you from ever "lecturing" for the entire lesson. Although group leaders will constantly shape conversation, clarifying and correcting as needed, they will probably not talk for the majority of the lesson. This study guide is meant to facilitate an investigation into biblical truth—an investigation that is shared by the group leader and the participants. Therefore, we encourage you to adopt the posture of a "fellow-learner" who invites participation from everyone in the group.

It might surprise you how eager people can be to share what they have learned in preparing for each lesson. Therefore, you should invite participation by asking your group participants to share their discoveries. Here are some of our tips on facilitating discussion that is engaging and helpful:

> ⟩ Don't be uncomfortable with silence initially. Once the first participant shares his or her response, others will be likely to join in. But if you cut the silence short by

prompting them, then they are more likely to wait for you to prompt them every time.

› Affirm every answer, if possible, and draw out the participants by asking for clarification. Your aim is to make them feel comfortable sharing their ideas and learning, so be extremely hesitant to "shut down" a group member's contribution or "trump" it with your own. This does not mean, however, that you shouldn't correct false ideas—just do it in a spirit of gentleness and love.

› Don't allow a single person, or group of persons, to dominate the discussion. Involve everyone, if possible, and intentionally invite participation from those who are more reserved or hesitant.

› Labor to show the significance of their study. Emphasize the things that the participants could not have learned without doing the homework.

› Avoid talking too much. The group leader should not monopolize the discussion, but rather guide and shape it. If the group leader does the majority of the talking, the participants will be less likely to interact and engage, and therefore they will not learn as much. Avoid constantly adding the "definitive last word."

› The group leader should feel the freedom to linger on a topic or question if the group demonstrates interest. The group leader should also pursue digressions that are helpful and relevant. There is a balance to this, however: the group leader *should* attempt to cover the material. So avoid the extreme of constantly wandering off topic, but also avoid the extreme of limiting the conversation in a way that squelches curiosity or learning.

› The group leader's passion, or lack of it, is infectious. Therefore, if you demonstrate little enthusiasm for the material, it is almost inevitable that your participants will likewise be bored. But if you have a genuine excitement for what you are studying, and if you truly think Bible study is worthwhile, then your group will be impacted positively. Therefore, it is our recommendation that before you come to the group, you spend enough time working through the homework and praying, so that you can overflow with genuine enthusiasm for the Bible and for God in your group. This point cannot be stressed enough. Delight yourself in God and in his Word!

✖ desiringGod

If you would like to further explore the vision of God and life presented in this book, we at Desiring God would love to serve you. We have hundreds of resources to help you grow in your passion for Jesus Christ and help you spread that passion to others. At our website, desiringGod.org, you'll find almost everything John Piper has written and preached, including more than thirty books. We've made over twenty-five years of his sermons available free online for you to read, listen to, download, and in some cases watch.

In addition, you can access hundreds of articles, listen to our daily internet radio program, find out where John Piper is speaking, learn about our conferences, discover our God-centered children's curricula, and browse our online store. John Piper receives no royalties from the books he writes and no compensation from Desiring God. The funds are all reinvested into our gospel-spreading efforts. DG also has a whatever-you-can-afford policy, designed for individuals with limited discretionary funds. If you'd like more information about this policy, please contact us at the address or phone number below. We exist to help you treasure Jesus Christ and his gospel above all things because he is most glorified in you when you are most satisfied in him. Let us know how we can serve you!

Desiring God
Post Office Box 2901
Minneapolis, Minnesota 55402

888.346.4700
mail@desiringGod.org
www.desiringGod.org